Gate to Chinese Calligraphy

Written by Guo Bonan

Foreign Languages Press Beijing

First Edition 1995

Translated by He Fei
Designed by Li Shiji

ISBN 7-119-01435-8

Published by Foreign Languages Press
24 Baiwanzhuang Road, Beijing 100037, China
Distributed by China International Book Trading Corporation
35 Chegongzhuang Xilu, Beijing 100044, China
P.O. Box 399, Beijing, China

Printed in the People's Republic of China

Contents

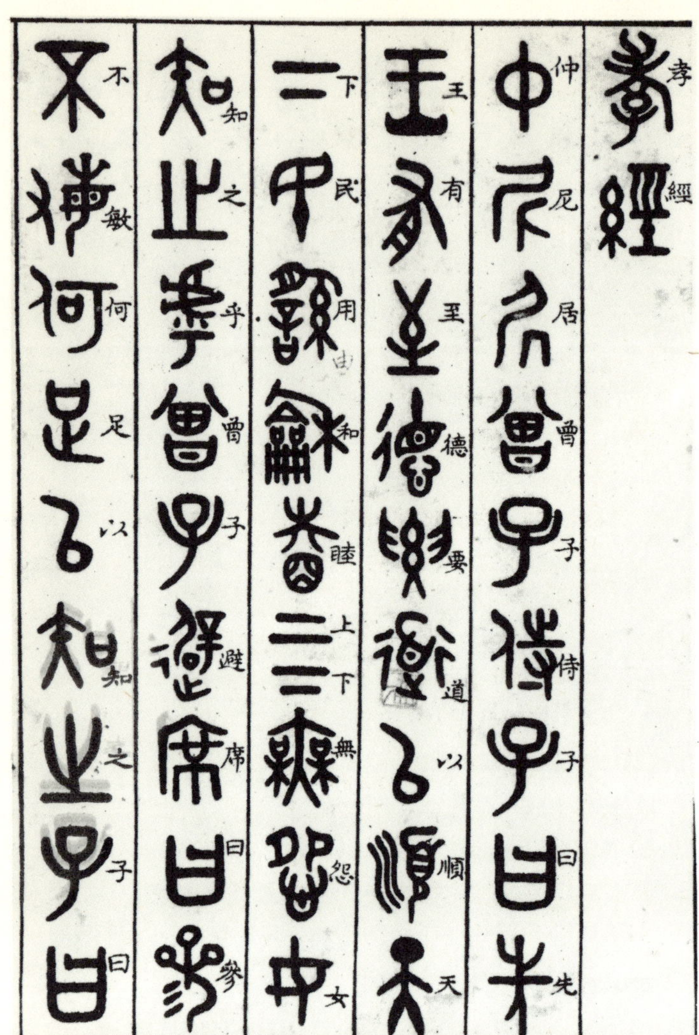

Wu Dacheng (Qing Dynasty). Portion of the *Classic of Filial Piety* (seal script).

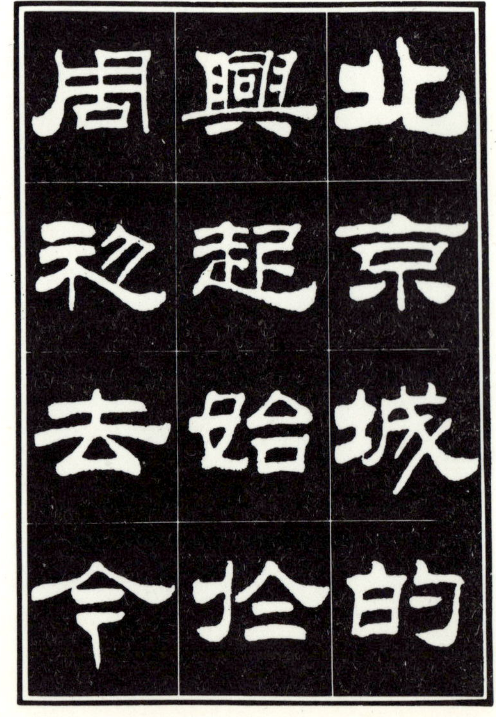

Liu Bingsen (contemporary). "On Repairing Beijing's Ming Dynasty City Wall" (classical script).

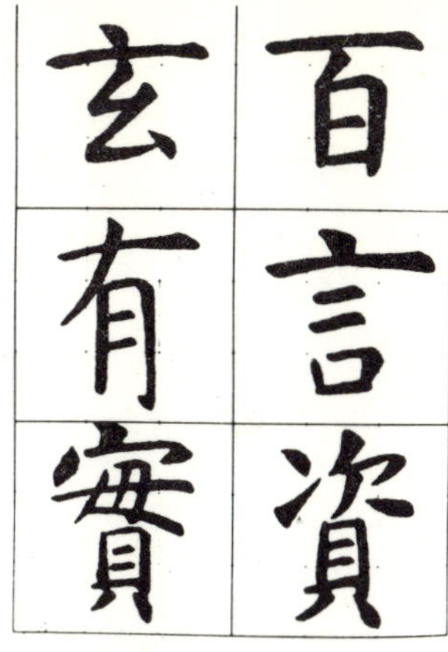

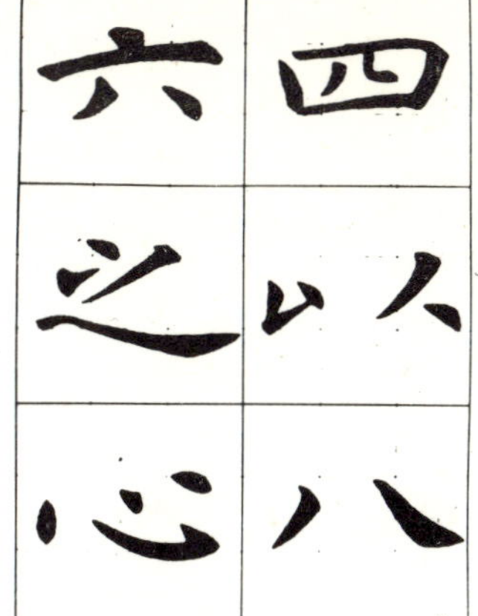

Zhuo Chengde (contemporary). Copy of the Stele in the Confucian Temple (regular script).

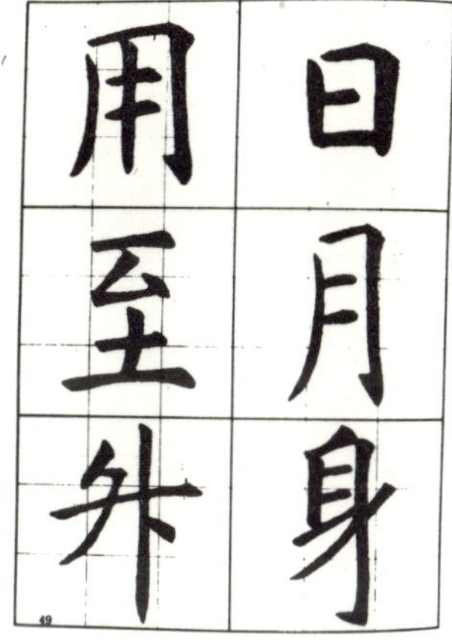

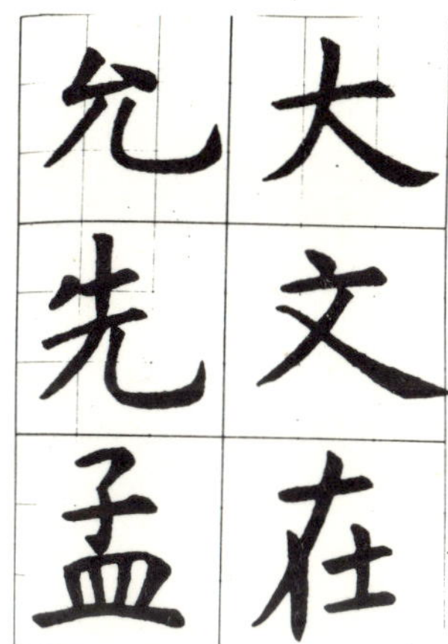

Huang Tingjian (Song Dynasty). "*Song Feng Ge*" (Pine and Wind Pavilion) (running/regular script).

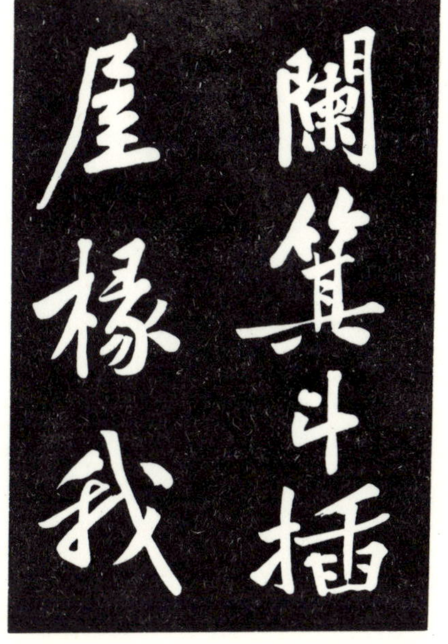

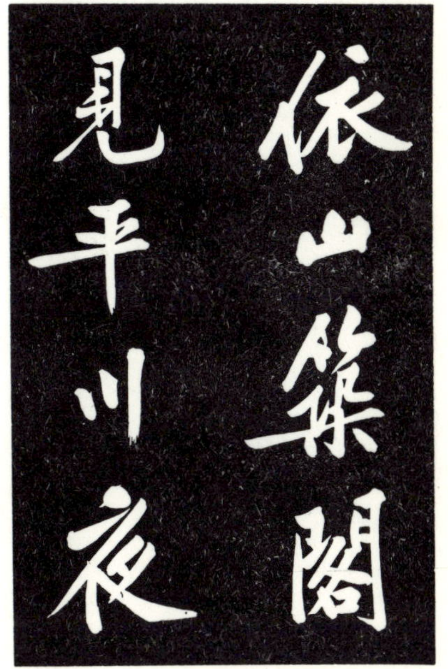

永和九年歲在癸丑暮春之初會
于會稽山陰之蘭亭脩稧事
也群賢畢至少長咸集此地
有崇山峻領茂林脩竹又有清流激
湍暎帶左右引以為流觴曲水
列坐其次雖無絲竹管弦之
盛一觴一詠亦足以暢敘幽情
是日也天朗氣清惠風和暢仰
觀宇宙之大俯察品類之盛
所以遊目騁懷足以極視聽之
娛信可樂也夫人之相與俯仰
一世或取諸懷抱悟言一室之內
或因寄所託放浪形骸之外雖

Wang Xizhi (Jin Dynasty). "*Lan Ting Xu*" (Preface to The Literary Gathering at the Orchid Pavilion) (running script).

茶香酒熟田千畝雲白山青水
一灣若是老天容我懶
暮年來共白鷗閒 [illegible]
[illegible]
[illegible]
[illegible] 板橋鄭燮

Zheng Banqiao (Qing Dynasty). "*Zi Shu Shi*" (poem in the author's own hand) (running/cursive script).

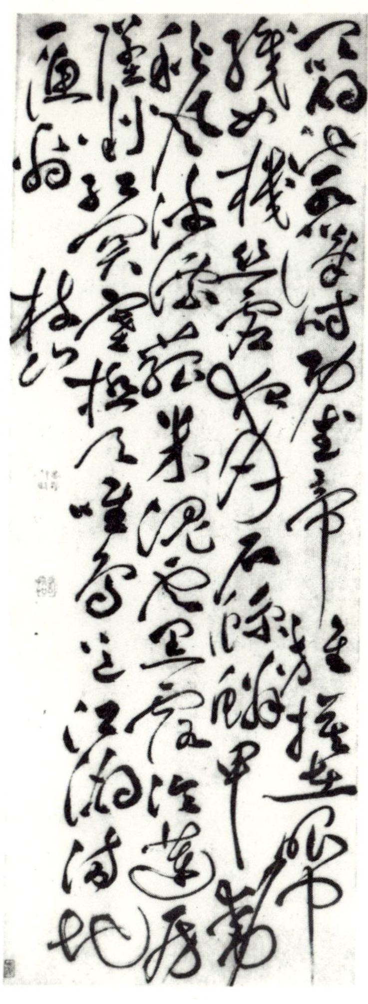

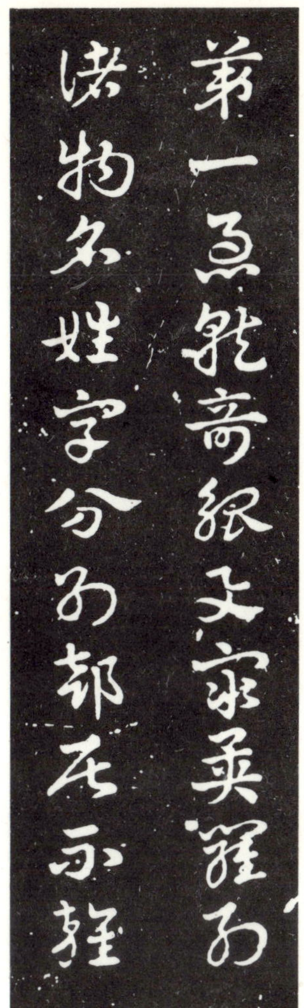

Shi You (Han Dynasty). "*Ji Jiu Zhang*" (seal cursive script).

Zuo Zhishan (Ming Dynasty). "*Qiu Xing*" ("Autumn Comes", a poem by Du Fu), (cursive script).

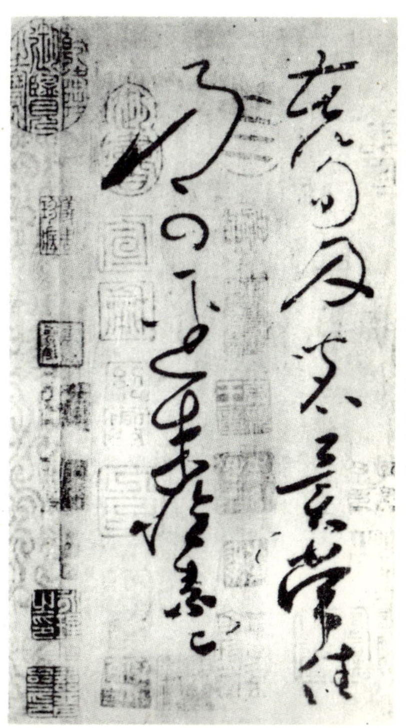

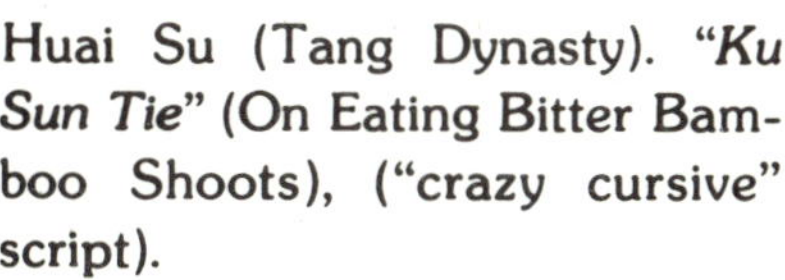
Huai Su (Tang Dynasty). "*Ku Sun Tie*" (On Eating Bitter Bamboo Shoots), ("crazy cursive" script).

1. What is calligraphy?

Chinese calligraphy is an Oriental art. But what makes it an art?

It is very much like painting. It uses Chinese characters to communicate the spiritual world of the artist. Just as one thousand persons will have as many faces, one thousand persons will have as many differences in handwriting. Through the medium of form, way of handling the brush, presentation, and style, calligraphy as a work of art conveys the moral integrity, character, emotions, esthetic feelings and culture of the artist to readers affecting them by the power of appeal and the joy of beauty.

Calligraphy is not only a practical technique for writing Chinese characters, but also a unique Oriental art of expression and a branch of learning or discipline as well. As a branch of learning it is rich in content, including the evolution of writing styles, development and rules of technique, history of calligraphy, calligraphers and their inheritance in art, and evaluation of calligraphy as a work of art. This branch of learning is wide ranging and deep, forming an important part of Chinese culture.

Like chopsticks, this calligraphy used to be wholly Chinese. As Chinese culture spread to Korea, Japan, Vietnam and Singapore, calligraphy became a unique feature of Oriental art.

A Japanese friend once remarked with pride that Oriental culture has one more art than Western culture, by which he meant that language in the East is not mere symbol, but a lofty art—Oriental calligraphy.

Recently knowledgeable friends in the West have discovered the unique beauty of Chinese calligraphy. They say every character is written like a beautiful flower. Western scholars visiting China develop a keen interest in and love for Chinese calligraphy. They study Chinese characters, and from the construction of the characters they seek to understand calligraphy. From calligraphy they seek to learn about Oriental culture. There are artists in the West who understand the abstract beauty of Chinese calligraphic art. They believe that Chinese calligraphy is the most ancient and most condensed of abstract arts. They praise this form of Chinese art as having the beauty of image in painting, the beauty of dynamism in dance and the beauty of rhythm in music. Thus abstract art—the ultramodern art of the West—takes cognizance of the most ancient art—calligraphy—of the East, establishing an intimate relationship between the two. Although calligraphy's home is China, it does not belong exclusively to China. It does not belong exclusively to the East, either. It's no exaggeration to say that calligraphy is a gem in the world's art treasury.

With a history of four to five thousand years, the art of calligraphy is rich and profound in content and has attracted the attention of artists the world over. The author of this booklet finds it difficult to treat the subject adequately or well in the limited space available, so he will confine himself to a brief discussion of the method and rules of regular script in Chinese calligraphy.

2. Analysis of Chinese characters

Calligraphy is the art of writing Chinese characters. To understand calligraphy, one must first know something about Chinese characters. The various nationalities in the world have created their own languages, but the Chinese have created an independent calligraphic art. Why? The reason is mainly related to the features of the language.

Languages fall into two systems; one expresses sound; the other expresses meaning. The cuneiform writing of the Sumerian, the Katakana in the Japanese language, English, French, Russian, German and Latin—these languages are phonetic. The language of the sacred books of ancient Egypt, the pictographic language of Crete, the Chinese language and the language of the Dongba nationality are all ideographic.

Ideographic languages have for the most part become extinct. Only one such language, Chinese, is still widely used today. A comparison of the two systems of language indicates that a phonetic language has an advantage over an ideographic language. Alphabets with few letters can easily be learned and memorized. Such a language can be popularized more easily. The *pinyin* form of Chinese represents the direction of language development. An ideographic language has a great many symbols. The morphology is cumbersome and difficult. It is hard to learn and remember it. Such a language cannot easily be popularized.

The inscriptions on bones and tortoise shells of the Shang Dynasty, three thousand years ago or so, had vocabularies of five thousand symbols. The recently published *Han Yu Da Zi Dian*, a comprehensive Chinese-language dictionary, has over 54,000 entries. So vast is the Chinese vocabulary! Every character can be written in regular script, grass script, official script, etc., and every script can be written differently, ranging from a few to as many as scores of styles. The largest runs to about one hundred. For example, *bai shou tu* shows one hundred ways to write *shou* (longevity) in official script.

The Chinese language contains an enormous number of characters. A Chinese who spends his entire life learning to write his language will find it difficult to complete his task. The difficulty facing the novice can hardly be imagined.

Everything in the world is said to have a dual character. If it possesses advantages, it will also have drawbacks. This is also true to language. In the case of Chinese there is a huge stock of characters and the morphology varies greatly. This means that you can write words in many ways. The drawback is thus turned into an advantage. It opened up a huge vista for Chinese calligraphy to develop into an independent art. Chinese characters may be difficult to master, but they are governed by rules. Just like notes in music, characters are formed by changing the combination of elements. Tens of thousands of words in Chinese can be broken down into several hundred component parts. Take, for instance, the two characters *Zhong Guo* (China). The character *zhong* 中 is made up of 口 and a vertical stroke 丨. The character *guo* 国 is made up of 口 and 玉. Further analysis of Chinese characters leads to the discovery that there are eight basic strokes: namely, dot (丶), dash (一), perpendicular downstroke (丨), downstroke to the left (丿), wavelike stroke (㇏), hook (亅), upstroke to the right (㇀) and bend (㇇). The eight basic strokes, like notes in music, can be developed into many "tunes" and "movements", or schools of Chinese calligraphy.

Every Chinese character can be said to contain a picture. The two characters 旦 and 暮 show sunrise and sunset. In primitive pottery inscriptions 旦 was written as [illegible], made up of 日 (sun), 月 (moon), and 山 (mountain), showing that the moon had gone down behind a mountain and that the sun is rising. The character 暮 was written as 莫 in ancient script. In official script it is written as [illegible]. 屮 indicates grass. 茻 indicates a thick growth of grass. The picture shows that the sun has set behind a thick growth of grass. It is not too much to say that these two characters are pictures of sunrise and sunset. The reason why Chinese calligraphy has developed into an art containing images may be closely related to the fact that a picture stands for a word. Some will perhaps remark that Chinese calligraphy is the art of the brush. This is true. If you use a stiff or hard pen, it is difficult to write such beautiful characters as done by the brush. If you try to use a brush to write the twenty-six letters in the *pinyin* system, it is also difficult to create such beautiful images as in Chinese calligraphy.

Examine how the following characters are constructed:

England	英	艹 央	加	力 口			Canada
	格	木 各	拿	合 手			
	兰	丷 三	大	一 人			
U.S.A.	美	𦍌 大	希	乂 布			Greece
	国	囗 玉	腊	月 昔			
Clinton	克	十 兄	约	纟 勺			Johnson
	林	木 木	翰	十 早	人 羽		
	頓	屯 頁	逊	子 小	辶		

3. Four treasures of the study

To write Chinese characters, you need a brush, ink, paper and ink stone, commonly referred to as the four treasures of the study. In order to learn calligraphy, it is necessary to learn about these tools, select them carefully and take care of them. As the saying goes, one must temper the means to achieve the end. This is by virtue of necessity.

Brush

The brush was invented by Meng Dian (?-210 B.C.), according to legend, yet primitive painted pottery had decorative designs painted by tools more or less like a brush. Clearly visible stains or marks of a brush were left in certain places on the pottery. From this it may be surmised that the brush predated the written language itself. The history of the Chinese brush can be traced back at least six thousand years.

That Chinese calligraphy has become an art that enjoys a worldwide reputation is in a large measure related to the use of the brush to write the characters. The head of the brush is made of the hair of the goat, wolf, rat or rabbit, which is softer than bamboo, pencil, quill or ball pen. Because of its softness its written strokes can be light or heavy, thick or fine. The strokes flow naturally, entering an artistic world with an element of wonder. Other materials may give you a handsome style, but they can hardly attain the level of achievement in calligraphic art executed by the brush.

Writing brushes are soft, stiff or a combination of the two. A soft writing brush is flexible and easily moistened with ink. Made of goat hair, it is called *yang hao* in

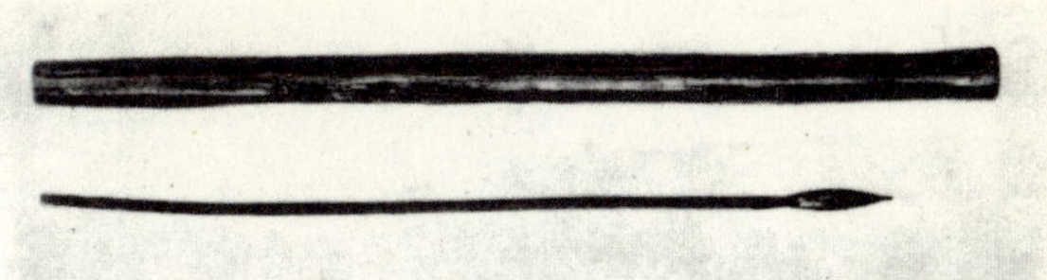

Brush and brush holder

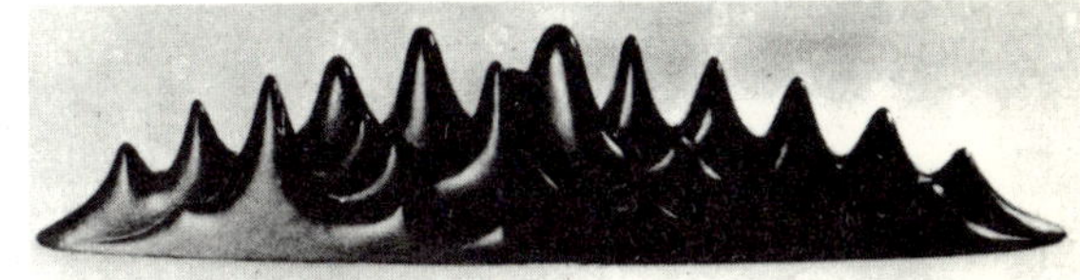

Brush rest

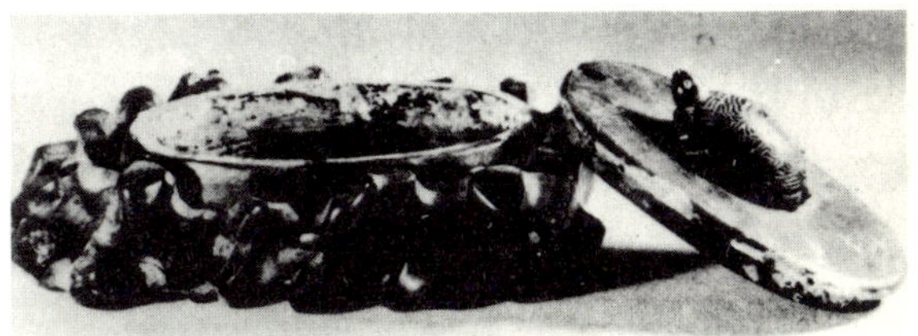

Brush washer

Chinese. Some calligraphers think beginners should use this brush to practice handwriting, since it facilitates forceful writing. Practice begins with medium-sized characters, however, which call for regularity and neat lettering. Thus it is advisable to use a combination writing brush, since it is difficult for the beginner to handle a goat-hair brush.

Stiff brush

This brush is stiff and hard and does not hold a large amount of ink. Made of wolf hair, it is commonly called a wolf-hair brush. To practice writing small characters, which call for regularity and neatness, it is better to use a stiff brush.

Jian hao, or a combination of stiff and soft hair, contains goat hair and the hair of another animal. Rabbit hair is somewhat purple, so a rabbit-hair brush is called a purple brush. The ratio of hair may be 70

percent rabbit hair and 30 percent goat hair or vice versa or 50 percent of each. *Zi yang jian* is the name in Chinese for a rabbit-goat writing brush.

Selecting the writing brush

The Chinese brush may be big or small, stiff or soft. The important thing is that it serve your own practical purpose. Generally, a big, soft brush is used to write large characters and a small, stiff one to write small characters. The point must be "round like an awl" that can be "pressed like a chisel". The Chinese brush point should have the following characteristics: roundness, pointedness, evenness and strength. Roundness means the point should be rounded and robust. Pointedness means it should be as sharp or pointed as an awl. Evenness means that when you spread the brush and hold it down, the brush is even. Strength means the point is flexible or elastic. You can moisten a new brush in your mouth, then press it forward and backward on your thumb. The brush will go round and round smoothly. When you pick the brush up, it will return to its former shape naturally becoming as sharp and pointed as before. This means your brush is all right.

Protecting your brush

A new brush has a sticky coating that must be removed by immersing the brush in warm water (do not use hot water). The hair will then fluff out. Do not try to remove the glue by force. Do not use your teeth to remove the glue. The glue on brushes for writing small characters should be removed from two fifths of the length of the hair. The glue on brushes for writing medium-sized characters should be removed from half the length of the hair, and the glue on brushes for writing big characters should be removed from two thirds the length of the hair. It is not advisable to remove all the glue from the brush. If it is removed entirely, the brush will not have the required force or rigor. How much glue should be removed just depends on the convenience of the user.

The brush for writing big characters must be washed in clean water after use. Be sure no ink is left on the brush, which should be carefully groomed. The brush should be hung up with the tip downward. The brush for writing small characters must be put in a sheath after use, to protect it from gluing up. If the brush is not used for a long time, it must be kept in a box or a bag. Camphor balls should be used to protect the brush from being moth-eaten.

Ink stick

Legend says that Xing Yi first invented ink stick about 2,800 years ago, yet archaeologists have detected ink marks on the back of inscribed bones or tortoise shells of the Shang Dynasty, 3,200 years ago. There are many varieties of ink stick. The most famous is *hui mo* (Anhui ink stick), made from the pines that grow on Huangshan (Yellow Mountain) in Anhui Province. The trees are burned and the soot left after burning makes excellent ink stick. Xi, a famous ink maker, moved to Shexian County in Anhui at the end of the Tang Dynasty (618-907). His method for making ink stick from pine soot was handed down to later generations. Such a ink stick has enjoyed a good reputation for more than a thousand years. The Anhui ink stick has magic qualities. It is as hard as stone and does not deteriorate for as long as ten years. The ink produced from the Anhui ink stick is as black as black paint. Many charming stories and anecdotes about the Anhui ink stick have been recounted in literary circles, past and present. Ink sticks fall into three major categories, according to the chief materials

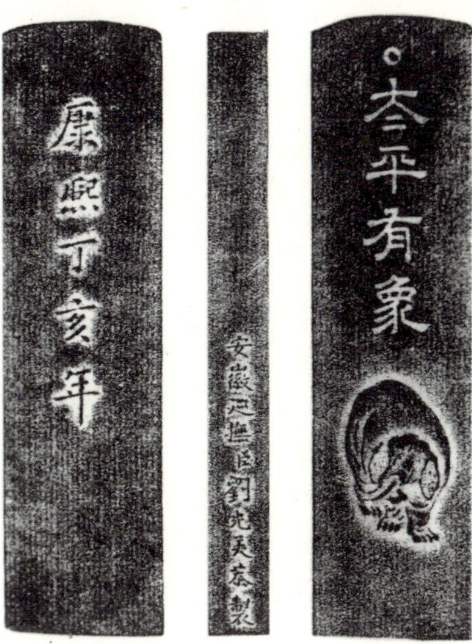

Rubbing from a *Tai Ping You Xiang* inkstick (Qing Dynasty).

used in manufacture. The pine-soot ink stick. This is made with the mixture of pine soot, which is the main part, a certain amount of glue, medicinal material and spices. The oil-soot ink stick. Tung oil, sesame oil, rapeseed oil or petroleum is burned and the soot is mixed with gelatine, medicinal material and spices. The oil- and pine-soot ink stick. This is a mixture of the previous materials for making the oil-soot ink stick and pine-soot ink stick. Proportions vary, and the quality of the ink stick differs accordingly.

Choosing the ink stick

The quality of the ink stick may be judged by its color and sound. Glossy purple is best. Black is second. Glossy green is third. Glossy white is last. If you strike the ink stick and it gives a light sound, this means it is a fine ink stick. If the sound is muffled, it is not a good one. If the sound is fine when you grind the ink stick on the slab, it means you have a good ink stick. If the sound is rough during grinding, it means the ink stick is none too good.

How to grind the ink stick

Clean water is used for grinding. The best water contains a small amount of salt. Next comes well water, then tap water, then distilled water. Do not use tea or hot water to grind an ink stick.

The ink stick must be balanced in the hand during grinding or rubbing. Press hard and rub lightly. Rub the ink stick slowly and evenly against the ink slab or ink stone in big circles. At first use only a little water. When a thick liquid forms, add water and rub or grind again. The thickness or thinness of the ink depends on how much or how little you need to use. If the ink is too thick, it will be difficult to use the tip of the brush, which will glue up. If the ink is too thin, it will probably filter through the paper.

You may use prepared liquid Chinese ink to write Chinese characters during ordinary practice sessions. This form of ink is very convenient. If the ink is too thick, pour out a small amount from the ink bottle, add water and rub. Don't pour

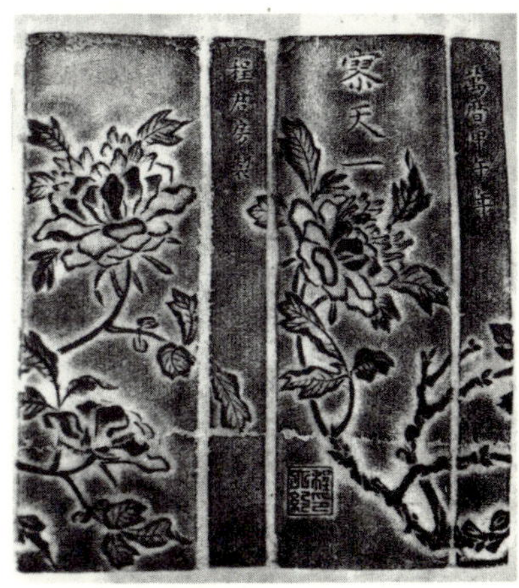

Rubbing from a *Cheng Jun Fang* inkstick.

water into the bottle of prepared liquid ink. You will only spoil the glue, which will stink. In learning calligraphy it is best that you rub or grind the ink stick on the ink slad or ink stone. If you use prepared liquid ink you will not enter the art world. Rubbing or grinding the ink stick against the ink slab or ink stone prepares you for practicing handwriting. During the rubbing or grinding you have time to study the specimen of writing that you intend to copy. This will enable you to make better progress in the course of time. So whenever you can, rub or grind the ink stick against the ink stone yourself.

Paper

Paper was invented by Cai Lun (?-121), according to legend. Archaeological discoveries reveal, however, that in the early Western Han Dynasty, or two hundred years earlier than the time of Cai Lun, a coarse paper made of hemp had already come into existence. Paper is of many kinds, but Xuan paper has been considered best throughout the ages for Chinese calligraphy. Xuan paper is produced in Jing County, Anhui Province. The county was under the jurisdiction of Xuanzhou Prefecture in the Tang Dynasty. Jing County paper was first shipped to Xuanzhou, then transshipped to other ports. That is why Jing County paper is called Xuan paper. The paper is soft and fine textured, suitable for conveying the artistic expression of both Chinese calligraphy and painting.

Xuan paper has good tensile strength and not easily eaten by moths. It can be preserved for a long time. It therefore has the reputation of lasting a thousand years. There are numerous kinds of Xuan paper, such as *dan*, *jia*, *luowen*, coral, tiger-skin

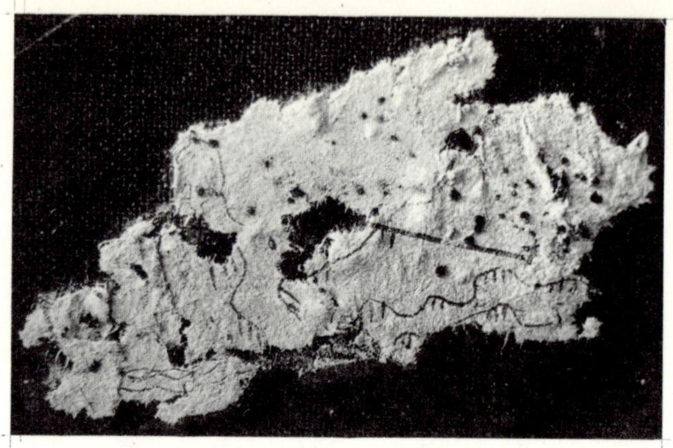

2,200 year old paper.

and jade-plate. Quality depends on whether the paper is unprocessed, processed or half-processed. Unprocessed paper absorbs water easily. Ink filters through this paper easily, too. Put your brush on this paper to make sure the thickness or thinness of your liquid ink is suitable. Processed paper goes through a process whereby gelatine made from bones and alum are added. This kind of paper does not absorb water easily. It is stiff or hard to the touch. Half-processed paper has a neutral character, in that it absorbs water, but it does not filter through easily.

Xuan paper for painting and calligraphy is rather expensive. Beginners can use coarser, rougher paper instead. More commonly used paper includes *yuanshu*, *maobian* and *baima*. It is not good to use too glossy a paper, such as *youguang* and *kaobei*. It is easy to practice forceful writing on coarse, rough paper, but not on glossy, smooth paper. Calligraphers in ancient China used to practice writing on stone slabs found by the side of a well, because it was difficult to obtain paper then. In the end they became good calligraphers. In modern times white-painted wooden boards, thin plastic film and plastic sheets are used as substitutes for paper to practice writing. You may erase the characters with a wet cloth and write again. You don't need to use paper, and the result is just as good. It's somewhat to your advantage to use coarse paper. If you practice handwriting under less favorable conditions, you develop greater adaptability. Do not think that you cannot produce good handwriting if you do not have good-quality paper to practice on.

Ink slab or ink stone

When the ink slab was invented is a rather controversial question. Ancient Chinese attributed the invention to the Yellow Emperor, yet the ink slab had been in use in primitive times, six to seven thousand years ago, two thousand years earlier than the era of the Yellow Emperor, to produce colors. Archaeologists have discovered many ancient ink slabs, such as a jade ink slab of the Shang and Zhou dynasties, a stone slab of the pre-Qin Dynasty, a painted slab and a painted slab mixed with sand belonging to the Han Dynasty, copper and silver slabs as well as iron slabs of the Wei and Jin dynasties, a blue porcelain slab of the Six Dynasties and a clay slab of the Tang Dynasty. Most ink slabs, modern or ancient, were made of stone. The earliest ink slab was made of stone and acquired the greatest popularity. Ink stones or ink slabs have been classified into three categories since the Tang Dynasty: Duan, She and Tao.

Duan ink slab

Produced in Zhaoqing, Guangdong Province, it is made of Duan stone, so named because the Duanxi River runs at the foot of Mount Fuke, where the stone is found. Said to be the best stone for making ink slabs, Duan stone was used to make ink slabs as early as the Tang Dynasty (618-907). Duan ink slabs have earned a high reputation among Chinese scholars ever since.

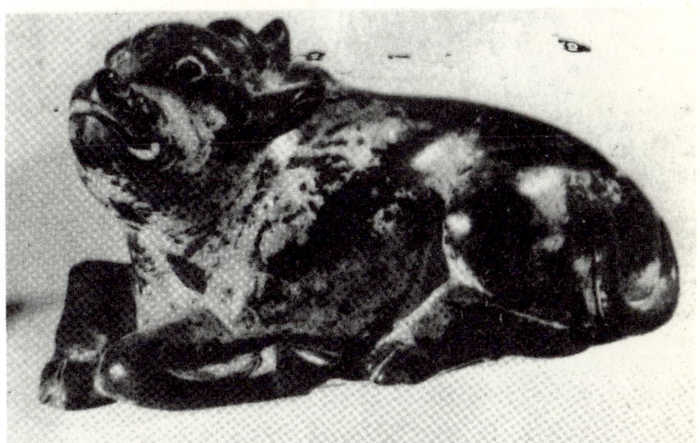

Carved stone paper weight.

She ink slab

It is named after Shezhou Prefecture, Anhui Province, where it was first produced in the Tang Dynasty. Many counties under the jurisdiction of this prefecture produce She ink slabs, but the best come from Mount Longwei, Wuyuan County, Jiangxi Province. Sometimes She ink slabs are referred to as Longwei ink slabs.

Tao ink slab

This ink slab has been produced in Taozhou since ancient times. Now it is produced mainly in Taoyan Village, Zhuoni County, Gansu Province. Tao ink slabs are made of stone found at the Tao River; hence the name.

One feature common to all three kinds of ink slabs is that the stone is hard and fine. Though hard, the stone is not dry. Though fine, it is not slippery. With a hard, smooth stone you produce liquid ink easily by rubbing the ink stick against the stone. Since the stone is fine, but not slippery, it yields ink very quickly.

Any stone not too glossy or slippery or too coarse or rough may be used by the

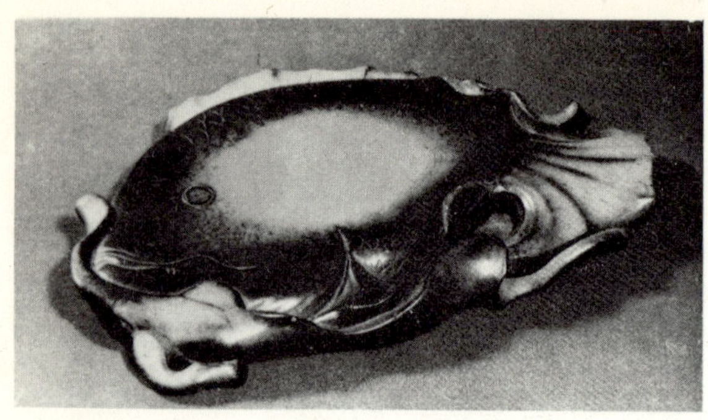

Chengni inkslab
(in sequential order in Chapter 3
to be positioned as appropriate)

beginner. The slab may have a cover, since a covered slab stores ink more easily. The ink will not blow away or dry up.

In grinding the ink stick against the ink slab exert your force evenly, so as to keep the ink slab steady. Grind only the ink you need for writing. After use, the slab must be washed clean. Leave a bit of clean water in the center of the slab. This will keep the slab in good condition. Take care not to stain the slab with oil or grease.

4. The way to hold the brush

To practice calligraphy, you must learn the proper way to hold the brush. This has much to do with the body's posture. You must hold the brush properly and also learn how to use your wrist and elbow while writing.

Body posture

Your posture while you write depends on the size of the characters you intend to write and your physical conditions. Proper posture will affect the speed of your progress and also your health. A contemporary calligrapher named Tang used the wrong posture, and though he became a calligrapher, he became a hunchback as well. He is called Tang the Hunchback.

What is the correct posture for writing? When sitting, the body should be erect, the shoulders balanced and the back straight. The legs should be apart, the feet evenly and firmly on the ground. The paper is held down by the left hand. The right hand holds the brush. The head is slightly forward, but be careful not to bow too low. Fix your eyes on the spot where you intend to write. Your eyes and the tip of your writing brush should be thirty centimeters apart. Your whole body should feel natural; do not pay undue attention to posture, or your body will become stiff or rigid. Correct posture simply prevents deformity of your body and enables you to write well. If you write characters larger than ten centimeters, you have to stand up and write. You may use any appropriate posture, depending on the situation.

Finger method

The important thing about holding the brush is the rational way of holding the five fingers and the coordinated use of these fingers. The functions of the five fingers are called *ye*, *ya*, *gou*, *ge* and *di* in Chinese.

Ye means to press down and refers to the use of the thumb. The thumb should press the brush slantwise from inside to outside. *Ya* refers to how the index finger holds the brush handle. Move the finger slantwise and bend it slightly from outside to inside. The index finger and the thumb coordinate, so that one presses and the other holds the brush handle.

Gou (hook) is the way the middle finger hooks the outside of the brush. Move this finger forcefully from left to right to hook the brush. The middle finger must coordinate well with the third finger to write characters. *Ge* refers to the way the third

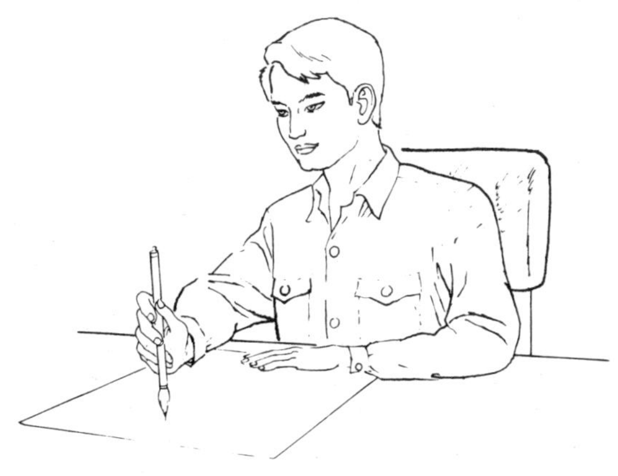

Proper posture for writing while seated.

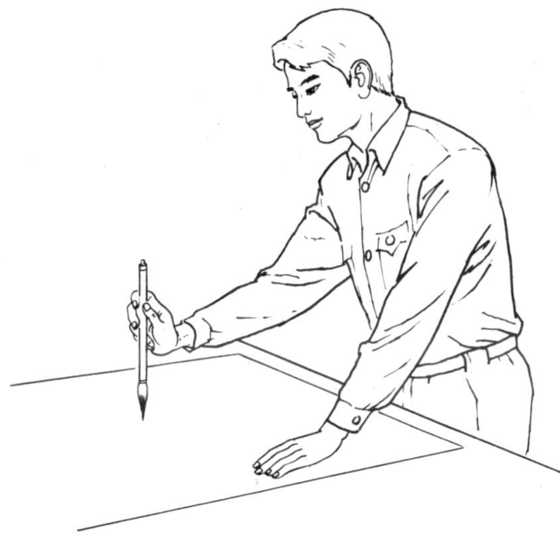

Proper posture for writing while standing.

finger press the brush. The third finger is placed on the inside of the brush handle pressing the handle from the inside to the outside. It coordinates with the middle finger, so that the two fingers exert an even and balanced force.

Di refers to the work of the little finger, which is placed under the third finger to help it.

The important points in holding the brush are: The fingers must exert substantial force. The palm does no actual work. Xu Chengyi, a calligrapher, recommends the following:

The tiger's mouth is like a crescent moon.

The palm is shaped like hiding an egg.

If the five fingers coordinate with each other,

The movement of the brush will be agile.

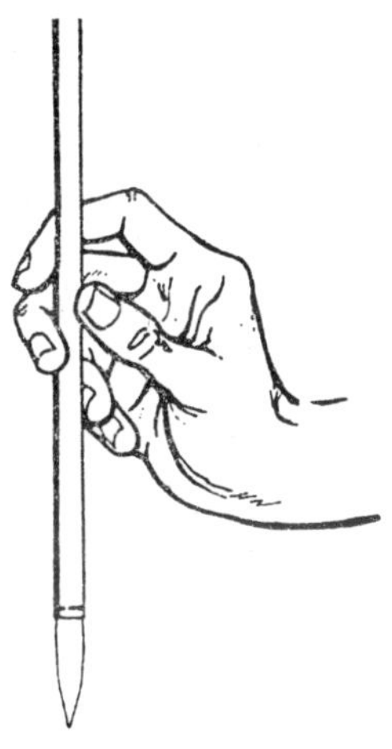

Holding the brush.

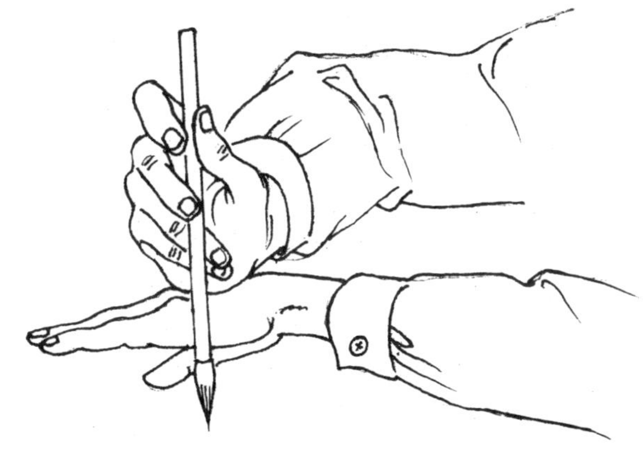

Supported wrist method.

Method of using the wrist

Besides the fingers, one must use the wrist and elbow to write Chinese characters. The wrist is crucial and must be used with agility. You use the wrist to manipulate the tip of the brush. The four positions of the wrist are: rest, cushion, lift and suspend.

Rest the wrist of your right hand on the table. This will enable you to use your fingers well. Employ this method when you are writing very small characters—as small as the head of a fly, the Chinese say.

Cushion the wrist of your right hand. Usually you cushion it with your left thumb or your left wrist. This lifts your right wrist. This method is very often used for writing ordinary small characters.

Lift your right wrist from the table. Some people also call it suspending the wrist. It is used to write medium-sized characters.

The last position is to suspend both the wrist and the elbow. Neither touches the table. This method is used to write big characters.

These four wrist positions are only relative. If you intend to raise your calligraphy to the level of art, you must practice the suspended-wrist position from the very beginning. Would-be calligraphers must not be afraid of difficulty. They must acquire this basic skill.

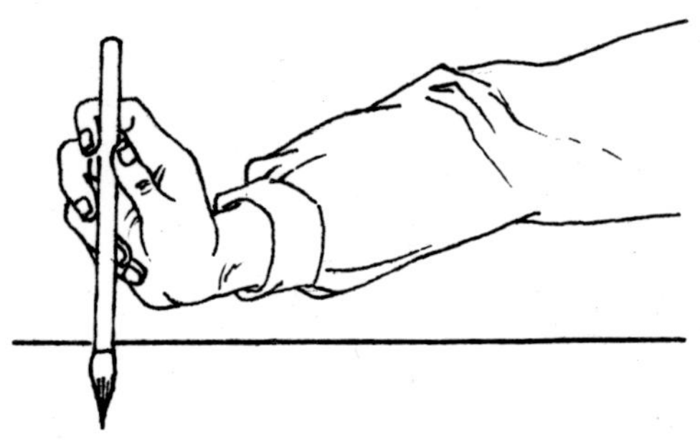

Raised wrist method.

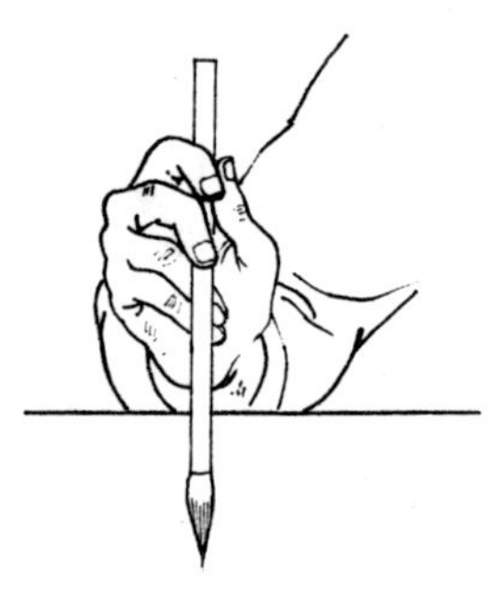

Suspended wrist method.
(in Chapter 4)

5. Essentials of writing technique

Writing technique in a broad sense includes the way to hold and use the brush to write characters. There are countless ways to wield the brush. I shall dwell only on the basic ways.

The Chinese term *qi bi* literally means to begin your stroke. The term *shou bi* means to end your stroke.

In writing characters each stroke involves *qi bi* and *shou bi*. If the stroke of a Chinese character is regarded as the basis of word construction, *qi bi* and *shou bi* are essential steps that determine the form of your stroke.

You must not make indecisive strokes —not knowing how you are going to write the strokes and where they are leading to. It will also not do if the strokes become unrecognizable—if the forceful strokes can't be told from the light strokes. If you are indecisive in writing strokes in calligraphy, your characters will be like withered trees, formless or styleless. The beginner will not be able to master the technique, but must pay due attention to the technique. Some people have been writing Chinese characters for several decades and still don't know the technique of *qi bi* and *shou bi*. They tend to neglect the technique. It is necessary to focus attention on it as you begin to write characters and cultivate good habits in writing strokes as you go along.

The basic approach to *qi bi* is: If you want to write a horizontal stroke, you must hold the brush perpendicularly to begin with. To do a perpendicular stroke, begin it horizontally.

The basic approach to *shou bi* is: When you end your perpendicular stroke, you must make the stroke appear like dew about to drop. When you end your horizontal stroke, you must proceed to the right and then come back to the left. This process is repeated each time.

Lift and press the brush

When you write words on a piece of paper, you don't use the same force all the time. You first lift the brush up, then press it down. Writing involves an alternate process of lifting up and pressing down. Sometimes you do it with a heavy hand, sometimes lightly. The characters appear heavy or fine. You may do a stroke with a hook or do a downward stroke slanting towards the right. In this way the strokes give viewers a sense of rhythm. The idea conveyed through the dot or the dash will come to life. The style of the calligraphy will appear on paper.

Zang feng and *lu feng*

What is *feng*? The tip of the brush has a central part of sharp, long hair (the main part), and its surrounding part of shorter hair. If you spread the hair evenly, you will see under sunlight that the tip of the main hair is transparent. This is called *feng* —the tip of the brush. It also means the cutting power of your brush. The term *zang feng* refers to first and last touch of the brush tip on the paper hidden in the writing stroke. In *qi bi* or *shou bi* you do not reveal these touches. This enables the cutting power of the brush to be kept in the strokes of the characters. The *zang feng* stroke imparts a suggestion of power, not revealing all that is in the mind of the calligrapher. This is what the ancient Chinese call sparing your cutting power in order to contain you energy or vitality.

Lu feng, in contrast, means a deliberate revelation of the cutting power of your brush, providing viewers with a sense of sharpness. This is what the ancient Chinese describe as revelation of the cutting power of the brush to give free rein to the spirit.

The *zang feng* method of wielding the brush means you turn the point in the direction opposite the one intended. For example, if you want to write a stroke from left to right, begin it by pressing the brush point to the right and then moving your brush a bit to the left to write the stroke to the right. End the stroke by returning a bit to the left. The cutting power of the brush will then be contained within the stroke.

Lu feng means the tip of the brush does not come from the opposite direction. You don't keep the cutting power of the brush within the stroke. The cutting power is revealed outwardly.

Zhuan feng and *zhe feng*

Zhuan feng is used to write a round dot. This calls for nonstop turning of the brush. Just let the tip of the brush go round and round. The dot will not become a square. Make a turn and it will be round, ancient Chinese said. This is what is meant by the term *zhuan feng*.

Zhe feng is used to write square strokes. The Chinese term *zhe* means to twist or bend. You break the line of your stroke to make a square, ancient Chinese said.

Zhong feng and *ce feng*

Zhong feng, or the central cutting power of the brush refers to keeping your brush point always in the middle of the stroke. In this way the strokes will be full and round, will have a three dimensional effect and will not appear plain. Ancient Chinese tended to overstress *zhong feng*, but they had a point there.

Ce feng means the writer uses the brush point one-sidedly or in a sidelong manner. The brush point is on one side of the stroke. Ancient Chinese described *zhong feng* as a means to exert vigor, while *ce feng* was a means to achieve elegance or beauty. A foremost calligrapher, Wang Xizhi (303-361), wrote his introduction to the *Orchid Pavilion* beautifully. The beauty of his calligraphy lies in his sidelong effect. Of course, he uses both *zhong feng* and *ce feng* as the necessity arises.

The ten writing skills mentioned above are not isolated. Related to each other, they form an integral movement. I have described them one by one only for the sake of convenience. Calligraphy is an art.

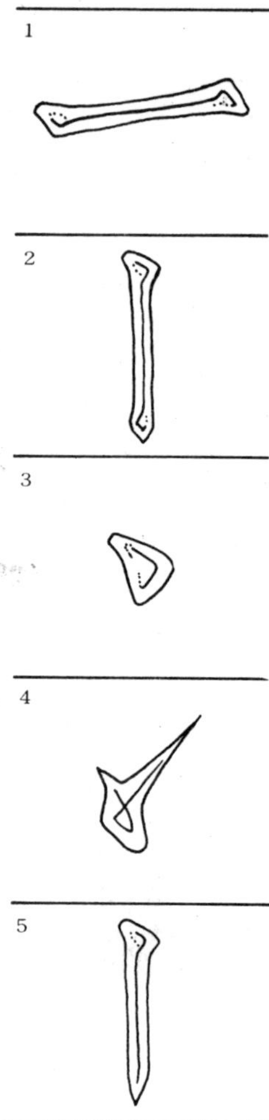

The skills, too, form an art. As such they are the result of long practice. It is difficult to describe their details or delicate points in words. In writing be sure to pay attention to each one and use them flexibly.

6. Eight kinds of brush stroke

Although Chinese characters total some fifty thousand, only six to seven thousand are used often. Despite the staggering number, analysis shows no more than eight basic strokes: dot (·), dash (—), perpendicular downstroke (丨), downstroke to the left, or left-falling stroke (ノ), wavelike stroke, or right-falling stroke (㇏), hook (亅), upstroke to the right (㇀), and bend or twist (㇇).

To learn calligraphy, it is vital that you learn to write the eight strokes before you learn to write Chinese characters. The strokes are the basic skill in writing. I shall attempt to explain something about these eight basic strokes, using as model the calligraphy of Liu Gongquan, found on rubbings from the stone tablet entitled *Xuan Mi Ta Bei*.

Dot

Take the Chinese character 唐 for example. To make the dot, move the brush slightly to the left (opposite direction) upward. Turn it to the right downward. Pause. Turn the brush slightly downward. Turn the brush upward. Turn the brush downward again. Slight pause. Now turn to the left and downward, as you end the dot.

There are many ways of writing the dot in Chinese calligraphy. Although the pattern remains the same, the dot assumes many forms. The learner must patiently study the various forms. He should compare the different forms and try to grasp their characteristics, mastering the way to write the dot with a Chinese brush.

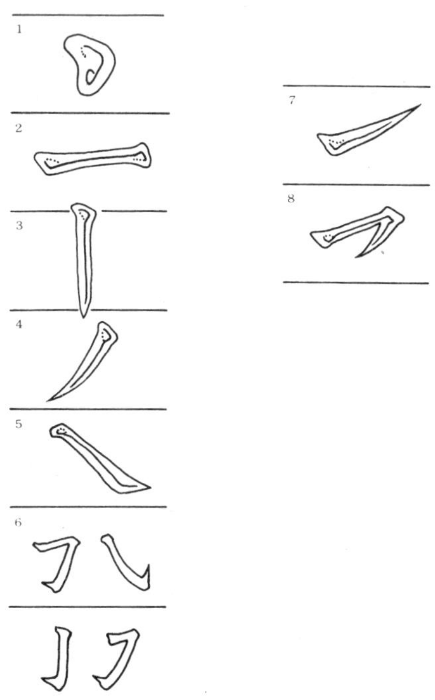

(1)
1.
dot
2.
dash or horizontal stroke
3.
perpendicular downwards stroke
4.
stroke downwards to the left or left-falling stroke
5.
stroke downwards to the right or right-falling stroke
6.
hook stroke
7.
stroke upwards to the right
8.
bend

Dash

The dash, or horizontal stroke, at the very bottom of the character 三 is a good example. Touch the tip of the brush on the paper and turn it to the opposite direction, the left a bit, as you begin writing. Tip the brush downward. Pause a little. Keep your brush point on the center of the stroke. Turn right. End the stroke. Pause. Turn the brush back to the left (see picture).

Perpendicular downstroke

Take the last perpendicular downstroke in the character 都 as an example. Begin the stroke by moving the brush to the left. Turn the brush to the right. Pause a little. Pull the *zhong feng*, or central part of the brush, down. When you are about to end the stroke, lift the brush a bit. When the point has reached the end, lift the brush. End the stroke by leaving a sharp

Examples showing brush movement in the Liu Gongquan style from the "*Xuanmi* Pagoda Stele."

点								
字例	唐	宗	必	初	欲	残	然	樂
横								
字例	三	仁	玄	法	江	集	悲	常
竖								
字例	都	骨	國	柳	西	師	帝	此
撇								
字例	人	大	殿	吞	於	凡	水	露
捺								
字例	人	文	入	之	趙	奉	林	度
钩								
字例	利	張	礼	慈	當	教	袋	机
挑								
字例	濟	滔	以	之	塔	括	厚	經
折								
字例	也	世	玄	尚	目	且	丘	毋

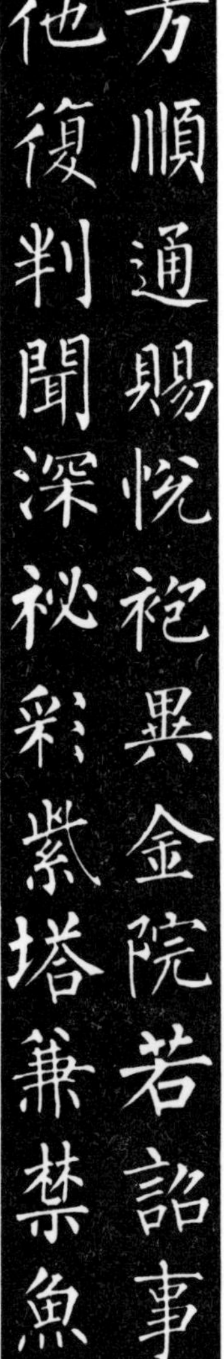

point on the paper (see picture).

Downstroke to the left

Take the left stroke in the character 人 for example. This stroke begins with a left upward stroke. Turn the brush to the right. Downward. Pause a little. Bring the *zhong feng* to the left downward. Lift the brush from the paper as you end the stroke (see picture).

Wavelike stroke

Take the wavelike stroke in the character 文 for example. Begin the stroke by moving the brush tip to the left upward. Bring the brush to the right and downward. A slight pause. Continue moving the brush to the right. Lift the brush when you end the stroke. It is like a wave, with three bends (see picture).

Hook

The hook may be of several kinds, such as the perpendicular hook in the character 有 or the crooked hook ㇂ in the character 武 or the *pao gou* in the character 气 or the *wan gou* in the character 易 .

The method calls for a pause when the brush curves to make the hook. Turn the brush around, then make the curve (see picture).

Upstroke to the right

Take the tick on the left part of the character 括 for example. Begin the tick with the brush moving to the left. Turn the brush downward. Pause. Now upward to the right.

When you write the stroke, you must be quick. There must be strength in your stroke (see picture).

Bend or twist

Take the first bend in the character 也 for example. Begin by moving the brush in the opposite direction—left. Turn the brush downward. Pause. The *zhong feng*, or the central part of the brush point, is to the right, upward. When you come to the bend, press the brush down. Lift the brush to the right slightly. Turn the brush downward. Slowly lift the brush to the left. End the stroke by lifting the brush from the paper (see picture).

This is a general description of the eight basic strokes in the Liu style of calligraphy. To study it in detail, refer to the book about Liu's calligraphy. Study and copy the strokes carefully.

7. Seven sequential steps in writing strokes

There is a proper sequence in the writing of strokes, with seven steps in the sequence.

The sequence in writing strokes was developed after long experience in calligraphy. The proper sequence facilitates writing. There are, however, exceptions to the rule. In the character 义 you may write the dot first or last. Both are right. Another example is the character 万 . You write the dash, or horizontal stroke, first, but how should you write the strokes below the dash: 丿 and ㇆ ?

According to the rule, from left to right, proper sequence should be: 一 丆 万 . However, if you write like this: 一 ㇆ 万 , it allows the blank sqace to be more evenly divided and looks more beautiful. In writing such characters you may be flexible. You don't have to follow the sequence of left stroke first, right stroke second.

Take another example: the character 右 . In running script in perpendicular lines you write the left-falling stroke first, followed by the dash, or horizontal stroke. You then write 口 . The order is as follows: 丿 一 口 .

When writing in horizontal lines, you write the dash, or horizontal stroke, first and add the left-falling stroke afterwards. The order is 一 丿 口 . Be practical. Facility comes first. You should follow the rules of sequence, but in doing so be flexible.

1. Three parts from upper to lower 三 意

2. Three parts from left to right 川 树

3. Three parts, first in the middle, then from left to right 小 山

4. Horizontal stroke(s) first, perpendicular stroke later 十 丰

5. Left-falling stroke first, right-falling stroke later 人 父

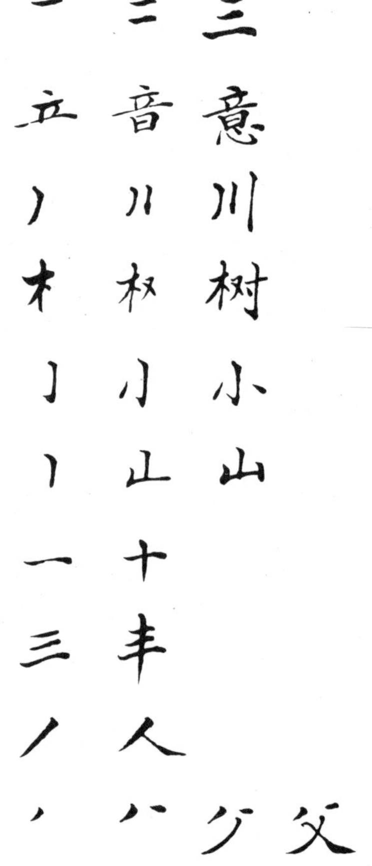

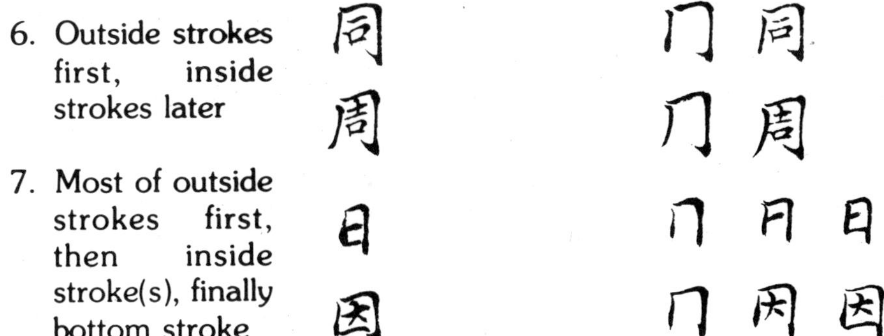

6. Outside strokes first, inside strokes later — 同 门 同; 周 门 周

7. Most of outside strokes first, then inside stroke(s), finally bottom stroke — 日; 因

Write the following characters using the stroke order indicated.

亚当　大卫　埃伦　卡尔

肯特　欧文　安娜　贝蒂

亚

当

大

卫

埃

伦

卡

尔

肯

特 ノ 𠂉 牛 牜 牜 牪 牪 特 特 特

欧 一 丆 又 区 区 欧 欧 欧

文 丶 亠 方 文

安 丶 丶 宀 宄 安 安

娜 𡿨 女 女 妇 如 娜 娜 娜 娜

贝 丨 冂 贝 贝

蒂 一 十 艹 艹 艹 艹 艹 苎 苎 苐 蒂 蒂

8. Structure of Chinese character —five essential points

Having studied how to hold and wield the brush and how to write the basic strokes, our next step is to study the structure of Chinese characters—arrangement, rational layout and formation of beautiful style. In architecture you need building materials, component parts, a building design, etc., in order to construct a high-rise building, a big hall or a palace. You must study the overall layout and the structure of different parts in the interior of the building. You must study its location and architectural style in the entire city as well. The same is true of handwriting. To study beautiful handwriting, you must study the arrangement of individual strokes—the structure. At the same time you must study the form of the whole character. The position and function of each character in calligraphy are its presentation.

Since ancient times Chinese calligraphers have laid stress on the rules of structure. Many writings have appeared on the subject. Each has its strong points. I shall give you a rough idea from my personal experience in handwriting. There are five essential points: *pingzheng*, *yunchen*, *rangjiu*, *xietiao* and *bianhua*.

Pingzheng

This term means the dash, or horizontal stroke, must be level, or flat, and the perpendicular downstroke must be exactly upright. This is the basic principle in word structure. To achieve this end, it is important to know the center of gravity of the character. If the center of gravity is balanced and steady, the form of the character can easily become *pingzheng*.

In the characters 平，王，本，山 the perpendicular stroke is the center of gravity. If you write this stroke well and place it in a suitable place, the center of gravity will be balanced and steady. The viewer will get a sense of balance from the character. Some characters are not balanced. They gravitate to one side, as in 多，也，易，乃. Yet there is still a center of gravity in each character. When you write it, the center of each character should be balanced. The strokes may lean to one side, yet the center is still balanced. The character 多 consists of two 夕, one placed above the other. The strokes tend to lean to one side, but the axis is the same. Take the character 也, for example. No stroke is exactly in the middle, but the short vertical stroke forms the center of gravity. The calligrapher Sun Guoting (c 648-c 703) once remarked that in studying layout the beginner should aim at *pingzheng*. *Pingzheng* is crucial in word structure.

Yunchen

This refers to the suitable arrangement of complicated and simple strokes, fat and lean strokes and long and short strokes in the same character. The suitable arrangement of these strokes gives one a sense of good balance and fine proportion. Take, for example, the characters 天，工，上，小. Each character has few strokes. You have to use heavy strokes and spread them out a bit. The characters 囊，爨，镳 have many strokes. The structure must be compact. The shape of the character must be slender and vigorous.

In the characters 三 and 卌 you find a repetition of horizontal and vertical strokes, three horizontal strokes in 三 and four vertical strokes in 卌. The distance between strokes is more or less the same. The long and short strokes are mixed. In writing 三 the first stroke must be heavy. The length of the stroke is in between. The second stroke must be short. The third stroke should be the longest, but thinner.

The Chinese term *yunchen* means well proportioned. The arrangement of long and short or large and small strokes gives the viewer a sense of harmony. This calls for a suitable arrangement of fat and lean strokes. The complicated and simple strokes must be well proportioned. *Yunchen* is the second important principle of word structure in the Chinese language.

Rangjiu

This refers to structural arrangement of the character. When you find an incongruity between left and right, top and bottom, large and small, tall and short, etc., you must try to make the part that is out of place with the rest less incongruous. Draw a distinction between the principal stroke and the subordinate stroke and harmonize them.

In characters such as 部，即，效，叔 the left side is taller than the right. Make the left side no more conspicuous than the right side.

In the characters ，炼，议，绩 the right side is taller than the left. Make the right side no more conspicuous than the left.

In the characters 敬，献，敛，勘 the left side is more complicated and larger than the right side. Make the left side no more conspicuous than the right.

In the characters 腾，峰，明，流 and similar characters that tend to be one-sided, the right side is complicated and the left side is simple. The right side is full. Make the right no more conspicuous than the left.

The same is true of top and bottom. Making the sides match is another principle in the structure of Chinese characters.

Xietiao

This term refers to harmony between thick and thin strokes, long and short strokes, and fat and slender strokes. It also refers to harmony in the same character between complicated and simple parts, tall and short parts, left and right parts and top and bottom parts. As in *yunchen* and *rangjiu*, the aim is harmony. Between different characters placed together there is also a question of harmony. One character may have only one stroke. The next character may have twenty to thirty strokes. Harmony between these neighboring characters must be considered. There must be harmony between characters with complicated strokes and characters with simple strokes. Consideration of this sort is beyond the realm of character structure. It is a matter of calligraphic layout and comes under the heading of presentation.

Next we come to the question of relationship of one stroke to another. Take, for instance, the characters 并 , 必 , 然 , 治 . There are two dots in the first character 并 . There are three dots and one left-falling stroke in 必 . There are four dots in 然 and three dots on the left side of the character 治 . Between the dots and other strokes there is the question of relationship. In 并 the two dots must relate to one another. In the character 必 the three dots and one left-falling stroke should relate to each other and form an integrated character. In the characters 北 and 非 the strokes face opposite directions. The short horizontal strokes on the left and right sides of 北 , and the short horizontal strokes on the left and right sides of 非 must relate to one another and become a harmonious unit. They are by no means unrelated. If we pay attention to structure and to the relationship of one stroke to another, we shall produce a harmonious atmosphere among the characters.

Bianhua

This term refers to flexibility in following the rules of calligraphy. For example, the character 林 is made up of two similar parts: 木 and 木 . However, because it is not suitable to write a right-falling stroke on the left-hand 木 , it is written instead as a dot. The character 森 has three right-falling strokes. If we write them as such, the character will not look nice. The writer uses a right-falling stroke only in the last 木 . Dots are used to write the other two 木 . Characters that have 木 in the lower part of their structure, such as 架 , 栾 , 桀 , 案 , replace the left- and right-falling strokes with two dots, left and right. This is flexibility, or *bianhua*, to make an appropriate change.

If the same character appears many times in one essay, a change is called for. Calligrapher Wang Xizhi wrote 之 twenty times in his preface to the *Orchid Pavilion*. Each time the character differs somewhat. This requires delicate skill. The master calligrapher tackled his task with great success. *Bianhua* in writting the same character appearing frequently in a piece of article is not a question of character structure, so the beginner is not required to make so many changes. Here I wish to emphasize only the importance of *Bianhua*. It is important to follow rules in calligraphy, but, more importantly, in following rules one must be flexible and not dogmatic. The ancient Chinese used to say a great master in calligraphy can teach people the rules of calligraphy, but he cannot make people skillful calligraphers.

Chinese calligraphers caution against three things. In learning arrangement, beginners are forbidden to write unbalanced or lopsided characters. In learning rules and regulations, learners are not allowed to be stereotyped or stagnant. Even when learners become mature calligraphers, they are forbidden to behave like raving maniacs or to adopt a vulgar style. The author of this booklet hope those who read it must exercise caution in learning. Remember: Follow the rules, but be flexible.

9. Process of practicing handwriting

The effective, traditional process of practicing handwriting consists of three steps: *mo*, *lin* and *xie*. *Mo* means tracing. There are two ways to trace: Trace the calligraphy printed in red in the copybook, or use the model in the exercise book to trace the character on semitransparent or transparent paper. *Mo* means to practice wielding the brush. You must acquaint yourself with the process of basic stroke writing and the order in which you write your strokes. In practice, attention should be focused on the strokes of your model, the structure and the style of calligraphy. This lays the foundation for the next step, *lin*, which is to put the model on the desk for you to copy. Deng Sanmu (1898-1963), a calligrapher, cautioned against tracing the model characters slavishly. You must study the structure of the character. Study the way it is written. Study the characteristics of the structure. In this way you will have some idea about writing it before you take up the brush. Mere copying without thinking leads nowhere. After a few months of study, proceed with the next step—*lin xie*.

Lin xie means that you have before you a specimen of writing—inscription on a stone tablet, etc. There are two steps in *lin xie*. You have before you a specimen of writing, then you make a copy of the specimen on paper with squares. You use this new copy as the model and copy the characters from it on paper also with squares. This is the first step of *lin xie*. After copying you compare the copied strokes with those in the model to see whether the positions of the former strokes are similar to those of the latter ones in the squares. This will make you acquaint with the characteristics of the form and structure of the characters.

The second step is to study the specimen, trying to memorize the strokes, then take it away. At first you may be able to

Huang Ziyuan's ninety-two methods for forming and structuring characters

間架結構摘要
九十二法

昔人论间架以有中画之字为式
论结构以无中画之字为式兹比
而合之不复区别

宇	宙	定	甯	天覆者凡画皆冒于其下
至	聖	孟	蓋	地载者有画皆托于其上
勑	部	幼	即	让左者左昂右低
讀	蝀	議	績	让右者右伸左缩
喜	吾	妻	安	横担者中画宜长

甲	平	干	午	直卓者中竖宜正
葡	萄	蜀	葛	勾拿法其身不宜曲短
句	勺	匀	匆	勾衄法其势不可直长
左	在	尤	尨	画短撇长
右	有	厷	灰	画长撇短
木	本	朱	東	画短直长撇捺宜伸
樂	棐	築	桼	画长直短撇捺宜缩
十	上	下	士	横长直短
才	斗	丰	井	横短直长

丕	正	亞	並	上下有画须上短而下长
目	自	因	固	左右有直宜左收而右展
川	升	邢	邦	右撇左直须左缩而右垂
伊	侈	僇	修	左直右撇宜左敛而右放
赤	赤	然	無	点复者宜偃仰向背以求变
三	冊	冊	聿	画重者宜鳞羽参差以化板
雖	願	顧	體	两平者左右宜均
御	謝	樹	衛	三合者中间务正
鑾	響	需	留	二段者上下平分中微加饶减

章	意	素	累	三联者头尾伸缩间仍要停匀
吸	呼	峰	峻	左旁小者齐其上
和	知	鈿	細	右边少者齐其下
嚚	囂	器	器	外四叠者体格必整方
齒	爾	爽	㡭	内四叠者布置宜匀密
此	七	也	乜	斜勒者不宜平平则失势
云	去	且	旦	平勒者不宜倚倚则无仪
丈	尺	史	又	纵捺之字必要擗头收尾
武	成	或	幾	纵戈之法最忌力弱身湾

恩	息	必	志	横戈不厌曲
勉	旭	魁	拋	伸勾贵抱持
天	父	外	丈	承上之乂正中为贵
鷀	鳩	輝	頫	屈勾之势退缩斯宜
鳥	馬	焉	為	马齿法其拿勾之锋宜注射四点之半
師	明	既	野	上平之字宜齐首
朝	故	辰	後	下平之字宜齐足
夔	談	茶	黍	重捺者须有缩有伸
禁	林	森	懋	叠趯者当或挑或驻

棗	戔	哥	柔	上下勾趯者下勾明而上勾暗
冠	冕	寇	宅	俯仰勾挑者俯勾缩而仰勾伸
雲	普	皆	齊	上占地步者听其上宽
衆	表	萬	禹	下占地步者任其下阔
施	騰	讓	靖	右占者右不妨独丰
敬	獻	斂	劉	左占者左无嫌偏大
弼	辨	衍	仰	右左占者中宜逊
蕃	筆	衡	擲	中间占者中独雄
鸞	鶯	鷲	釁	上下占者中小

風	鳳	飛	氣	纵腕宜曲劲
先	見	元	毛	横腕贵圆隽
庭	居	尹	底	纵撇恶鼠尾
友	及	反	皮	联撇恶排牙
參	修	須	形	三撇法以下撇首顶上撇之腹
治	洪	流	海	三点法以下点提锋与上点驻笔相应
是	足	走	辵	下字直母偏与上截中缝相对
者	耆	老	考	上字直母偏与下截左竖正对
馨	聲	繁	繫	错综者贵迎让穿插而恶纷纭

繼	纖	纏	纗	缜密者宜布置安排而嫌挤杂
車	申	中	巾	当悬针而垂露则无韵
卓	犖	單	畢	当垂露而悬针则无力
易	乃	毋	力	体虽宜斜而字心必正
正	主	本	王	形本自正而骨力必坚
身	目	耳	貝	字本瘦者其形勿短
白	工	曰	四	身本短者用笔宜肥
會	合	金	命	盖下之法撇捺宜均
琴	杏	各	谷	载下之势左右相称

土	止	山	公	虽宜肥而勿肿
了	寸	卜	才	虽宜瘦而勿臞
上	下	千	小	疏者丰之
贏	齋	龜	鼉	密者匀之
晶	磊	轟	森	堆叠者消纳之
爨	鬱	靈	糜	积累者清晰之
口	曰	田	由	下画宜微长以承右竖之末
丁	芋	宇	亭	末勾宜微拖似有带下之势
遠	邉	還	逮	之绕中字宜于上略大而下小

莫 矣 矢 契 | 画长撇短者右不宜用捺
作 仰 冲 行 | 左竖不嫌短右竖不嫌长
臣 巨 於 佳 | 左竖不嫌长右竖不嫌短
官 空 宥 宰 | 宝盖之勾如鸟之视胸乃妙
鷓 赫 鬭 鬻 | 排叠之画如工之镂物乃佳
卯 印 叩 卹 | 从卩之字准此
邱 郊 鄭 鄰 | 从邑之字准此
陼 隝 陔 阪 | 从阜之字准此
登 癹 發 癸 | 从癶之字准此

祭 蔡 察 登 | 从癶之字准此
乑 泉 衆 聚 | 从从之字准此
家 象 豪 豢 | 从豕之字准此
仁 儀 俯 休 | 单人傍字准此
従 徐 循 後 | 双人旁字准此
乳 亂 色 邑 | 从乙之字准此

光緒甲申長至前五日安化黃自元錄舊本

memorize only a few characters. Later you may memorize the entire specimen of writing. Now study the specimen again. Compare your own work with the specimen. This is a basic skill in calligraphy. Guo Moruo (1892-1978), a calligrapher, remarked that he could still remember every stroke in the calligraphy of Wang Xizhi in the preface to *The Literary Gathering at the Orchid Pavilion*, even though Guo was already over eighty years of age.

Xie

The aim in copying is to learn the basic method in handwriting. Once you have acquired this, you can practice handwriting independently by yourself. Your practice need not be confined to copying inscriptions from stone tablets. You may practice handling the brush and trying out the structure of a character and the style of calligraphy. Reassess these points and make some alterations. In the course of practicing over a long period of time you may be able to convey your ideas, reveal your character through calligraphy and create your own style. As I have said before, the initial practice in *lin xie* is to copy—copy the specimen—to make your writing similar or close. Afterwards you should emancipate your mind and become creative in a daring way. Depart from the specimen. Write in a way that will show your character and your own style. It is not easy. You must have your culture level and esthetic feeling raised to a higher level. You must practice the use of the brush, but you must acquire something beyond calligraphy. You must be skillful and follow the rules or methods of calligraphy, but you must envisage things beyond calligraphy, extending your horizon. This is rather important.

My personal experience in practicing handwriting tells me that the learner must accomplish four things: 1. Acquire skill in handling the brush. Be careful in observing the specimen. Copy the specimen, and make your writing look exactly like the specimen. Try to reproduce the specimen exactly, in both form and spirit. 2. Focus your attention on structure. The structure of characters in specimens by famous calligraphers differs. Each has its good points. Study these good points carefully and imitate them repeatedly so as to employ them in your handwriting whenever you write. 3. Try to master the technique of one school of calligraphy. Only when you have learned the good points of one school, can you absorb the good points of other schools. 4. Study diligently. Practice handwriting with perseverance. Only when you persevere, will you accomplish your aim. Wang Xizhi, the great calligrapher, used to say that with determination the learner could learn calligraphy in two months; the clever ones might spend one hundred days and acquire the basic skills. An ordinary Chinese saying goes, to write characters well enough, one hundred days spent in practice are quite enough. This means that it is not too difficult to write characters thoughtfully and correctly. A few months will be enough. To learn the rudiments of calligraphy is not too difficult. To be a calligrapher or an artist, the learner must persevere, spending a few years at least in learning his craft.

Jiu Gong Ge (nine palace square).

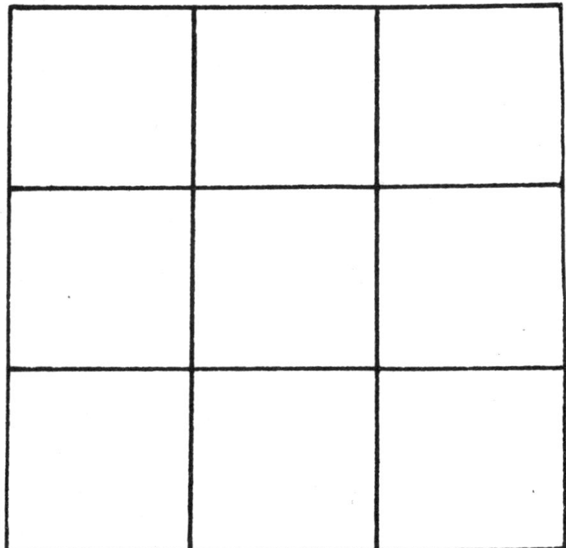

Mi Zi Ge (a copy book square divided into sections by the character *mi*, rice).

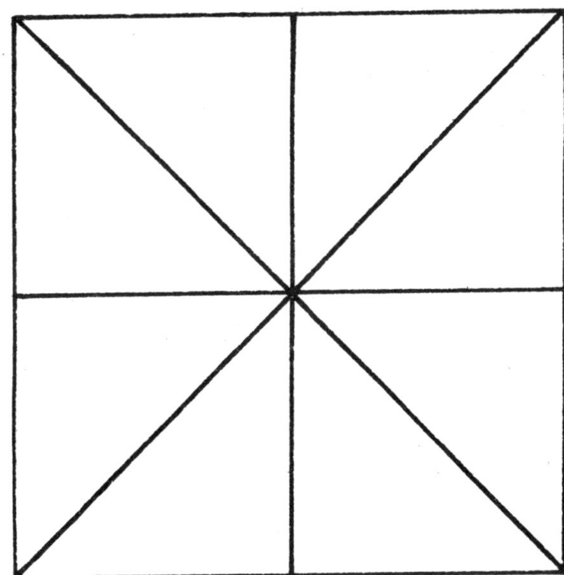

Hui Zi Ge (a copy book square resembling the character *hui*, return).

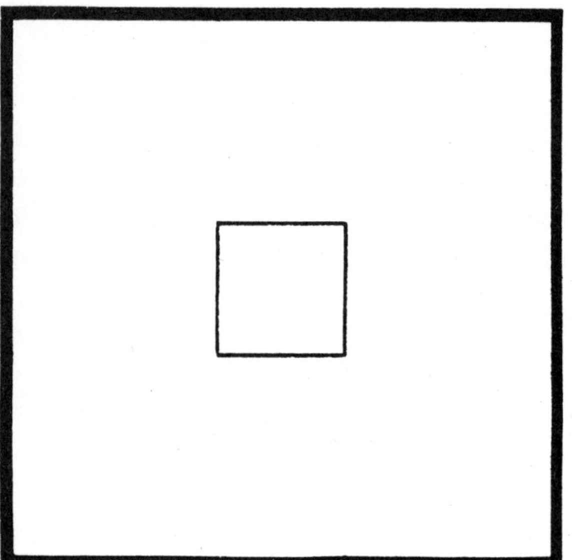

Tian Zi Ge (a copybook square resembling the character *tian*, field).

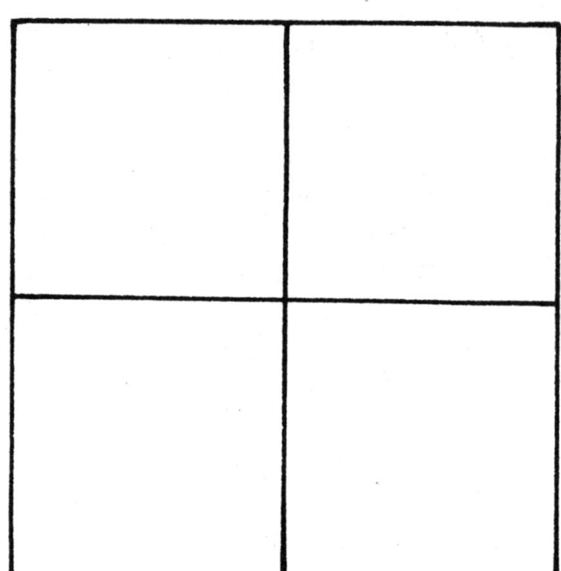

10. Elementary knowledge of rubbings from stone tablets

In learning calligraphy it is necessary to copy rubbings from stone tablets. How do we choose these rubbings? As a nation of calligraphers China has thousands of rubbings from stone tablets. Opinions may differ on the same stone tablet—praised by some and scorned by others. They are controversial. My own opinion is that the learner should choose rubbings of the four great schools of calligraphy—Yan, Liu, Ou and Zhao. The four have distinct features. The Ou school is marked by characters of strength. The Yan school produces characters with strong sinews or powerful framework. The characters of the Liu school are compared to the bones of the body. Zhao characters are compared to the flesh of the body. A description of each follows.

Yan style of calligraphy

Yan Zhenqing (709-785) was also known as Yan Qingchen. His ancestral home was Wannian, Jingzhao (now Xi'an, Shaanxi Province). He himself said that he was a native of Langya (now Linyi, Shandong Province). A prominent official in the Tang Dynasty, he was titled Duke of Lu Commandery. People respectfully called him Yan Lu Gong. He was a great calligrapher at the height of the Tang Dynasty's power and glory. An early representative work was *Duo Bao Ta Bei*. A fine work representative of his middle era was *Dong Fang Shuo Hua Xiang Zan Bei*. *Yan Shi Jia Miao Bei* was a powerful work representative of his later years. The style of his calligraphy is bold and vigorous, showing spaciousness and breadth.

Before Yan Zhenqing formed his own calligraphic system, most calligraphers had followed or imitated the calligraphy of Wang Xizhi and his son, Wang Xianzhi.

The Wang style is for the most part natural and unrestrained, elegant and refined. It can be compared to a romantic Chinese scholar or a classic Chinese beauty. Wang Xizhi's style is truly beautiful. However, it lacks strength and vigor. The atmosphere of Yan Zhenqing's calligraphy may be compared to the imposing appearance of a marshal, or it is as majestic as a sovereign ruler. The style has grandeur and loftiness. Like the poetry of Li Bai and Du Fu, Yan calligraphy embodies the grand spirit of the Tang Dynasty as its height. Yan calligraphy is as robust as the sun. After Wang Xizhi's time (Jin Dynasty) Chinese calligraphic art reached an epoch-making peak with the appearance of Yan Zhenqing's calligraphy. It became the fashion in the Song Dynasty to take Yan's calligraphy as a model for copying. This has persisted to this day, over a thousand years later.

There are many Yan-style rubbings from inscriptions on stone tablets. To copy small characters, get *Ma Gu Shan Xian Dan Ji*. To copy medium-sized characters, try the rubbing entitled *Duo Bao Ta Bei*. For big characters, try *Yan Shi Jia Miao Bei*.

Liu style of calligraphy

Liu Gongquan (778-865), alias Liu Chenxian, was a native of Huayuan, Jingzhao (now Yaoxian County, Shaanxi Province). A leading official of the Tang Dynasty, he was titled Duke of Hedong Commandery and popularly called Liu He Dong. A great calligrapher of his time, he was ranked alongside Yan Zhenqing as one of two great calligraphers. The two were referred to as Yan-Liu. Forthright, Liu had great integrity and was not careless. He was candid in giving his views. When the emperor asked him how one could write upright characters, he replied that it depended on the mind of the writer. When a man set the purpose of his life right, he would be able to write upright characters. On hearing this, the emperor's expression changed, as he thought that Liu was reprimanding him. This episode was described by later generations as calligraphically reprimanding the emperor. Liu Gongquan was speaking of the relationship between the mind and the brush. Before setting brush on scroll to paint bamboo, the painter must have the shape of the bamboo in his mind. In the same way a calligrapher sets his mind on the

Yan Zhengqing, Duo Bao Pagoda Stele

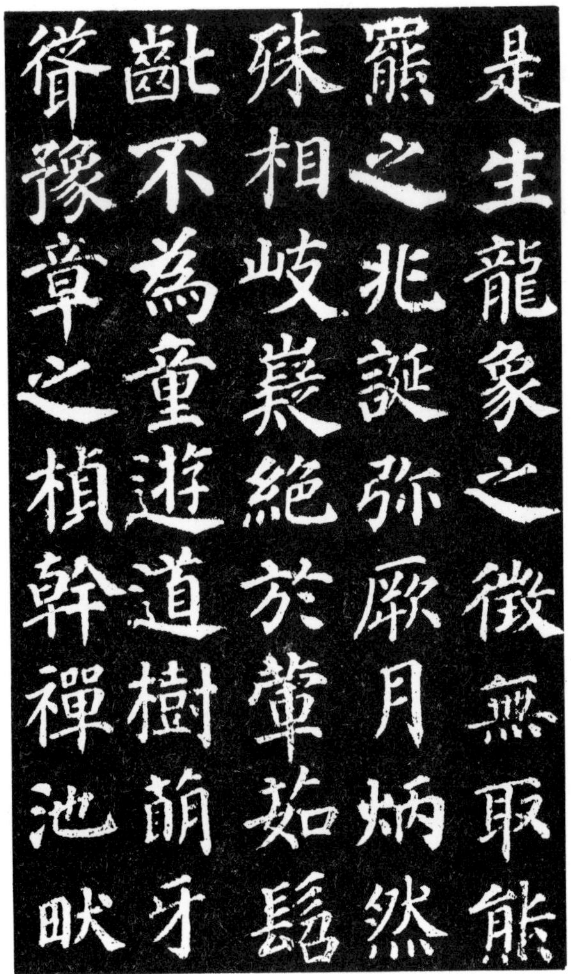

shape of characters before he actually writes them. This approach is common to both painting and calligraphy. The style of Liu calligraphy may be compared with the integrity of the calligrapher. The framework is very strictly executed. The style is strict and rigorous. Those wishing to imitate Liu's style in small characters may get copies of rubbings known as the *Diamond Sutra* and *Gui Lin Shi*. For medium-sized characters obtain a copy of the rubbing called *Tang Jian Yi Da Fu Bei*. For big characters *Xuan Mi Ta Bei* and *Shen Ce Jun Bei* are excellent specimens.

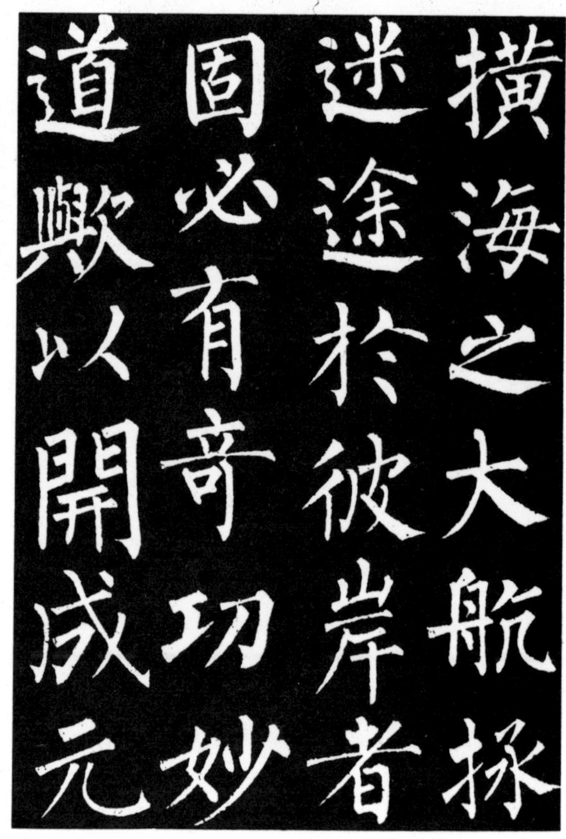

Liu Gongquan, Xuanmi Pagoda Stele.

Ou style of calligraphy

Ouyang Xun (557-641), also known as Xinben, was a native of Linxiang (now Changsha, Hunan Province). He was also a leading official of the early Tang Dynasty, serving the crown prince. The framework of characters in Ou calligraphic style is very rigid. His characters have strength, and his style has solemnity and grace. Recommended rubbings in Ou calligraphic style are: *Jiu Chen Gong Li Quan Ming*, *Hua Du Si Bei*, *Huang Fu Dan Bei* and *Yu Gong Gong Wen Yan Po Bei*.

Zhao style of calligraphy

Zhao Mengfu (1254-1322), alias Zi'ang and Xuesong Daoren, was a native of Huzhou (now Wuxing, Zhejiang Province). His style is mellow and full, handsome and rather refined, not at all vulgar. The structure is compact and well proportioned. We find flexibility that is rather natural. The running script is particularly graceful and elegant.

Sometimes the technique of writing in Zhao style appears to be more dexterous than required, resulting in lack of strength in the brush stroke. The calligraphy of Zhao Mengfu's later years is more mature, with vigorous strokes that display power.

Rubbings of inscriptions from stone tablets in Zhao style are as follows: *Dao De Jing* (in small characters), *Da De Fa Shi Bei* (in medium-sized characters), and *Dao Jiao Bei* and *Miao Yan Si Bei* (in big characters).

Of the four schools of calligraphy listed above Zhao style appears the easiest to learn. Beginners, however, with little basic skill, may find that their writing lacks strength if they start with Zhao style. This point should not be overlooked. If they begin their learning process by imitating Yan, Liu or Ou styles instead, they will gain strength in their writing. They may learn Zhao style later. This will enable them to add mellowness and fullness to their calligraphy. Their writing will have strength plus elegance. The bones will take on flesh, as it were. They will improve an already good script.

Apart from the four schools of Chinese calligraphy there are the works of Zhong You and Wang Xizhi, originators of regular script. Their works have won respect and high praise from calligraphers through the ages.

The above is elementary knowledge about rubbings of inscriptions on stone tablets used as writing specimens. Each school is different from the other and cannot be treated in the same way. The choice of rubbings depends on personal preference. No one can make decisions for you, for taste is a personal matter. You have to decide for youself. Choose the one you think you like best and you will achieve good results with half the effort. Otherwise, it will be half the result with twice the effort, as a Chinese proverb says.

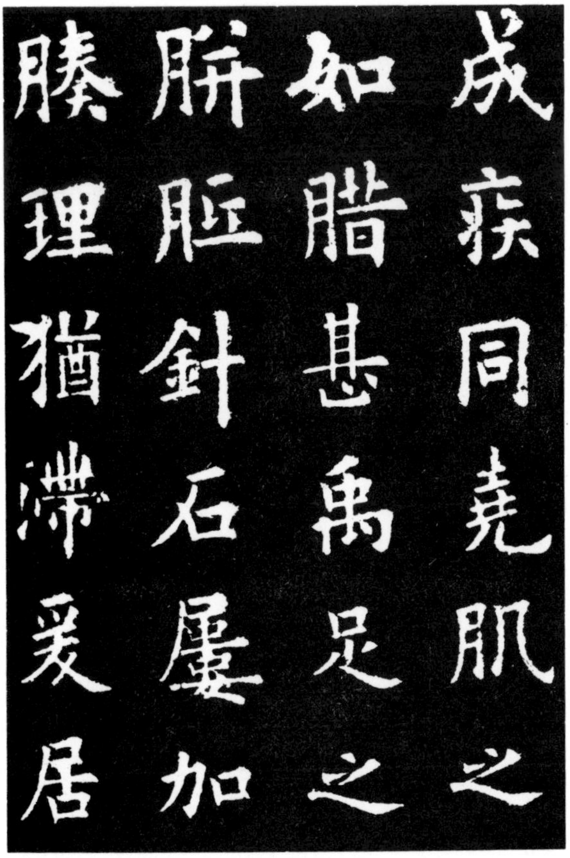

Ouyang Xun, Jiucheng Gong Liquan Ming, (Commemorative Stone Tablet for the Beneficent Spring near the Palace Jiucheng).

11. Origin of calligraphy

When did calligraphy originate? This question probably interests everyone who wishes to study calligraphy. No precise date is given in ancient Chinese history. Legend says that during the reign of the Yellow Emperor a man named Cang Xie invented the Chinese language. Calligraphy came after invention of the language. We may attribute the invention to 4,600 years ago, but this is only a legendary tale and may not be credible. What is interesting, however, is that archaeological discoveries since the birth of new China have authenticated that 4,500 years ago language came into existence in China. It follows that calligraphy entered an embryonic stage then.

In previous chapter on structure of Chinese characters I mentioned a sunrise painting. The painting was a design inscribed on a big-mouthed pottery jar—a sacrificial vessel to the sun by primitive Chinese forebears in Shandong during the period when the Dawenkou culture thrived.

This painting, or design, consists of three parts: upper, middle and bottom. The upper part is a round sun. Below it is a moon. A huge mountain with five peaks is at the bottom. The meaning of this painting, as explained by an expert in ancient Chinese language, is: Placing the moon below the sun shows that the moon

有膽略膂力過人方垂髫時即
從宣威隴蜀湖廣閒師行水陸
往来盤亘不啻萬餘里生長食

Zhao Mengfu, Memorial inscription for the tomb of Duke Zhang.

has gone down. The sun above the moon means the sun has just risen. The mountain with five peaks is Mount Tai, the highest of the five sacred mountains of China. So we are given a picture of the sunrise on Mount Tai. It is a primitive form of the character 旦. The same character appears in inscriptions on bone or tortoise shell, on ancient bronze vessels, in lesser seal characters, in official script and in regular script in later times. The origin of the character is the picture. From the angle of calligraphy we might regard the sun in the picture as round as a circle. The moon is a bit wavelike. The mountain is drawn with the brush exerting strength. The shapes of the moon and the mountain are well proportioned on left and right, imparting a sense of balance. The arrangement is small on top and big on the bottom. The top is round, the bottom flat. This gives one a sense of steadiness. As calligraphy, the character is well written insofar as technique, structure and presentation are concerned. The character has a strong rhythmic sense.

Let us look at another calligraphic work by primitive Chinese forebears—an inscription on pottery discovered in the ruins of the ancient Longshan culture in Dinggong Village, Zouping County, Shandong Province, in January 1992. There are five lines with eleven characters on the pottery piece. The lines seem to flow. The arrangement is good and well composed. The design on the Dawenkou culture pottery jar is a mixture of painting and calligraphy, difficult to distinguish, but the language on the Longshan culture pottery piece may be described as mature. To date, it is the most ancient calligraphic work in China. It may well be described as the embryo of calligraphy in seal characters. It is 4,300 years old.

Primitive written symbols.

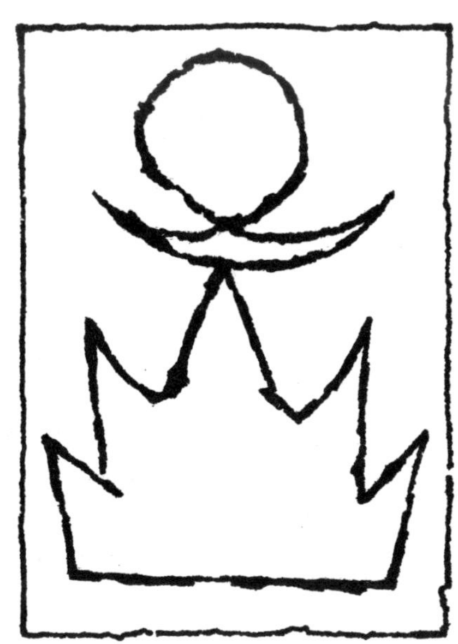

Characters inscribed on a pottery vessel, (Dawenkou Culture, c. 4000-2000 B.C.).

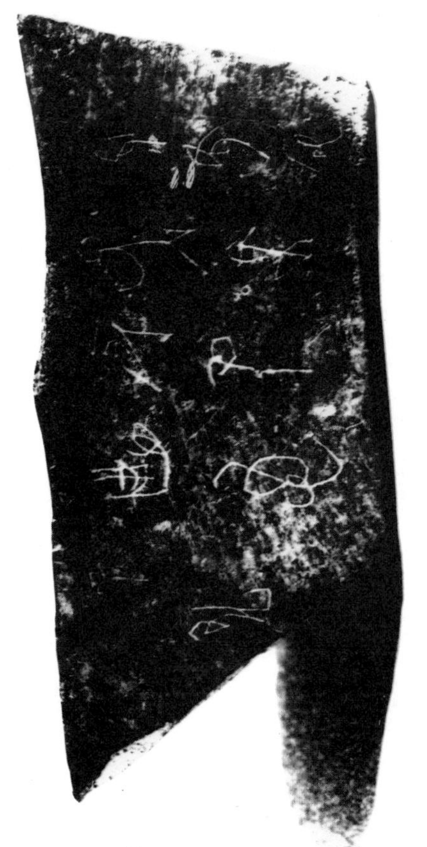

Inscription on Dinggongcun pottery.

Chinese calligraphy is at least four thousand years old, based on legendary tales and on textual criticism in archaeology.

The two primitive calligraphic works are both inscribed on pottery pieces by sharp tools. Therefore in the opinion of calligraphic historians they are the earliest works written by means of sharp tools—a sort of metal brush, or "hard" brush as the Chinese say.

It also shows that a metal tool was used earlier than the brush to write calligraphy in China. The inscriptions on bone or tortoise shell of the Shang Dynasty are outstanding examples of metal-tool calligraphy.

True enough, these inscriptions are

Clan insignia found on bronzeware

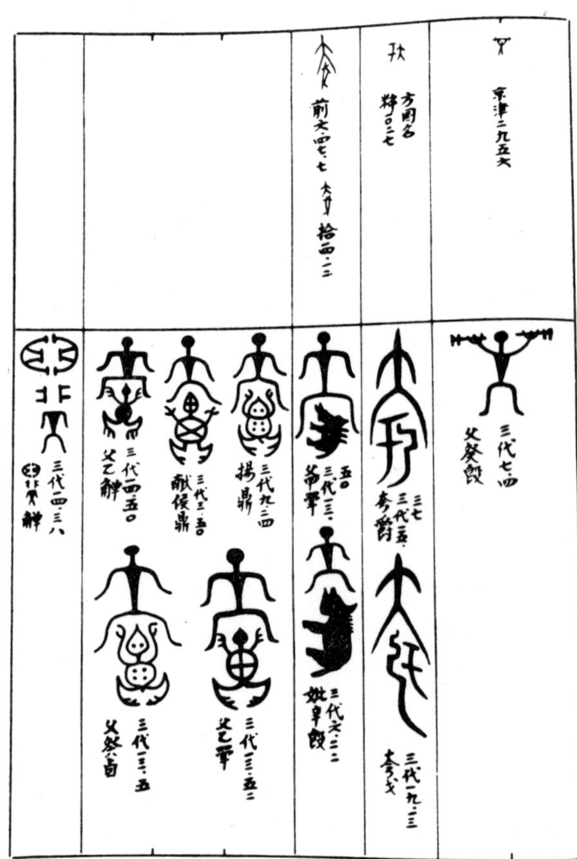

outstanding examples of ancient Chinese calligraphy written by means of a metal tool, but it would not be correct to say that all inscriptions on bone or tortoise shell were done by means of a metal tool. Before being inscribed with a metal tool, some were first drawn by a brush. They were inscribed on bone or shell later. The style of the calligraphy on the pottery piece in Dinggong Village is too complicated to have been inscribed directly on the pottery with a sharp tool. It is possible that something like a brush was used to write the calligraphy. In other words, calligraphy written by means of the brush also has a history of over four thousand years in China.

存七四一
三代三·五 父癸卣
錄遺四四 爵
乙七八二
后下五·二
三代八·六八 刀
三代六·七 父辛爵
三代四·六 且辛觚
摭一四七·三
三代五·0 刀爵
錄遺五四三 中戈

三代三·二 亞壺
三代四·三 觶
三代四·四 子壺
三代六·八 父辛爵
前六·三三·四
三代三·0 作父乙卣
同上
三代五·二 爵
摭一四一·六
簋帚二五
錄遺二六八 父辛觚
三代五·二七 己爵

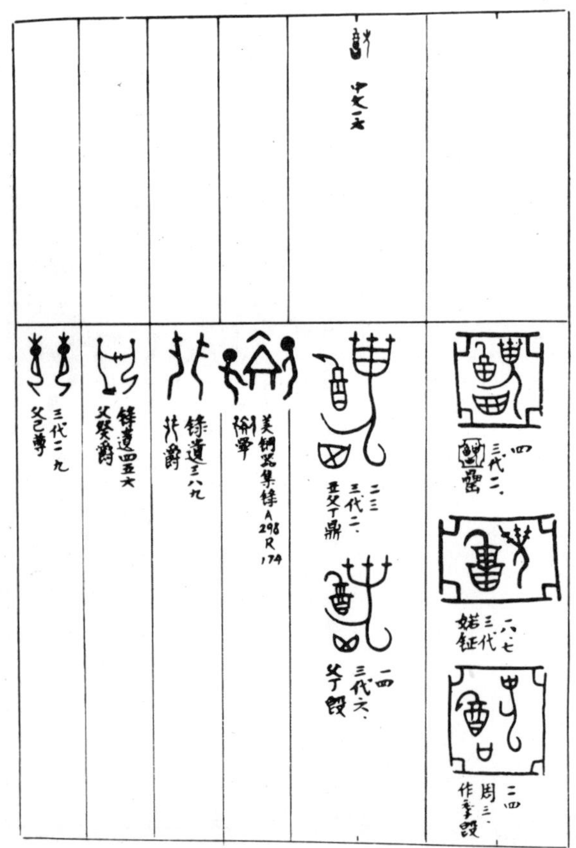
中文一·六
三代二·四 作彝
三代六·七 爵
周三·二四 作彝簋
三代二·三 父丁鼎
三代六·四 子簋
美帝國主義劫掠的我國殷周銅器集錄 A298 R174
錄遺三八九 爵
錄遺四五六 父癸爵
三代二·九 父乙尊

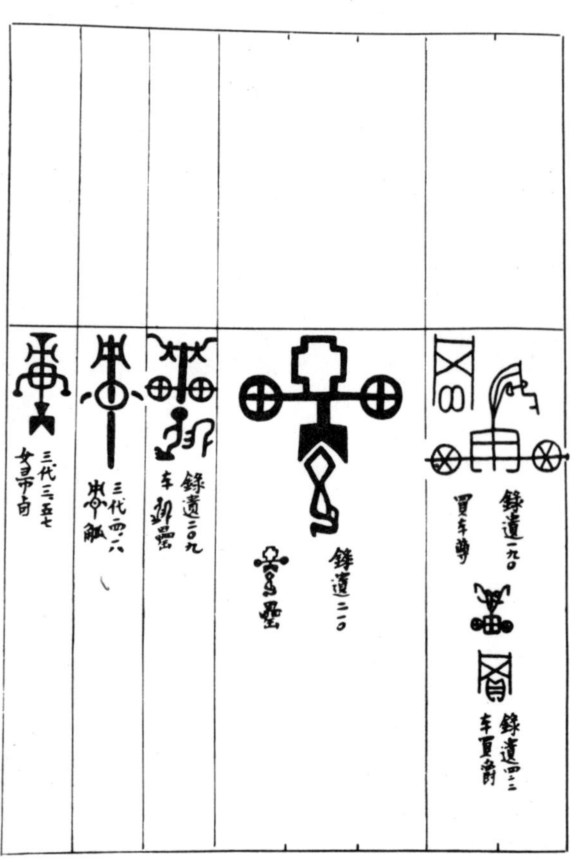
錄遺一九0 爵
錄遺四二 爵
錄遺二0 罍
錄遺二0九 罍
三代四·八 觚
三代三·五七 女卣

12. Changes in writing style

There are different writing styles, or scripts written by hand in the Chinese language. The breakdown in style is roughly as follows: *zhenshu* (regular script prevalent in the Han Dynasty), *caoshu* (cursive script), *lishu* (official script) and *zhuanshu* (seal character script). Chronologically, script style has experienced three epochs in the course of its over four thousand years of history. The three epochs are marked by three different scripts that came into fashion: seal character script, official script and regular script. The seal character period ran from the end of primitive society to the Qin Dynasty (221-206B.C.). The period, lasting more than two thousand years, is divided into three phases: early seal character, greater seal character and lesser seal character.

Early seal characters are characters written by primitive people, being the earliest form of writing on record. The inscription on the pottery vessel in Dinggong Village is an example of this. It has a mild

Oracle inscription on a tortoise plastrum, Shang Dynasty, (seal script).

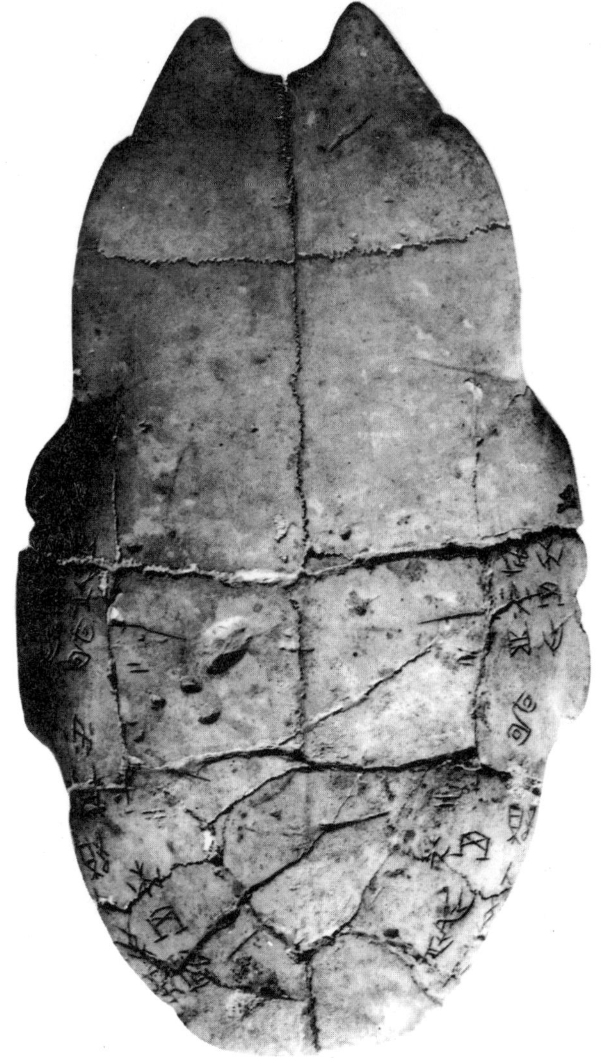

Inscription on the Mao Gong Ding (Tripod of Duke Mao), Western Zhou Dynasty, (seal script).

style and assumes varied postures. The characters look like a length of knotted rope. This form of writing was perhaps related to the use of rope by primitive people to record events. However, this point needs investigation.

Greater seal characters generally refer to ancient scripts of pre-Qin Dynasty, such as inscriptions on bones, tortoise shells, bronze vessels and drum-shaped stone blocks and the ancient language of the Six States.

Inscriptions engraved on bones and tortoise shells belong to the ancient language of the Shang and Zhou dynasties. Seal characters' feature is that strokes are carved in the round; however, the seal characters in inscriptions on bones and tortoise shells are mostly stiff and straight, because it is not easy to make a turn with the cutting edge of the tool in engraving. If we compare inscriptions on bronze vessels or hand script with inscriptions on bones and tortoise shells of the same period, we shall find that inscriptions on bones and tortoise shells have the attributes of the greater seal character script.

Early inscriptions on bronze vessels were first engraved on a clay mold and later cast on the bronze. Since it was easy to engrave on clay, the brush strokes showed roundness, fullness and roundabout turns. These features have been preserved to this day in vivid forms. Inscriptions on bronze vessels of later periods were engraved directly on the bronze with sharp knives or chisels. The characters became decorative, known as suspended-stitch seal characters.

Inscriptions on drum-shaped stone blocks were discovered in the early Tang Dynasty (around the year 618) in Shaanxi Province. The inscriptions were written in language of the pre-Qin period. They are famous works of calligraphy belonging to the period preceeding the Qin Dynasty and are in the collection of the Palace Museum in Beijing. Scripts of the pre-Qin period also include the ancient language of the Six States. They are all classified as greater seal character scripts.

Lesser seal character script was the officially approved script following the unification of Chinese languages by the Qin Dynasty. It is also known as Qin seal character script. Since it contrasts with the previous seal character script, the two are called greater and lesser. The Qin Dynasty used lesser seal character script to engrave inscriptions on stones extolling the merits of persons or things, to engrave seals or marks of authenticity or emblems or to write imperial edicts. It replaced greater seal character script, marking tremendous historical progress. For a country the size of China, where dialects are more numerous than in the various countries of Europe, a unified written language plays an important part as a link between various nationalities to cement national solidarity and achieve national unification. It was the Qin, or lesser, seal character script that served as a link and deserves much credit.

An outstanding work representative of Qin seal calligraphy is the writing of Li Si (?-c 208 B.C.), regarded as the father of lesser seal character script. He exerted a profound influence on the seal character script of later generations.

Oath of Marquis Ma, Eastern Zhou Dynasty, (seal script).

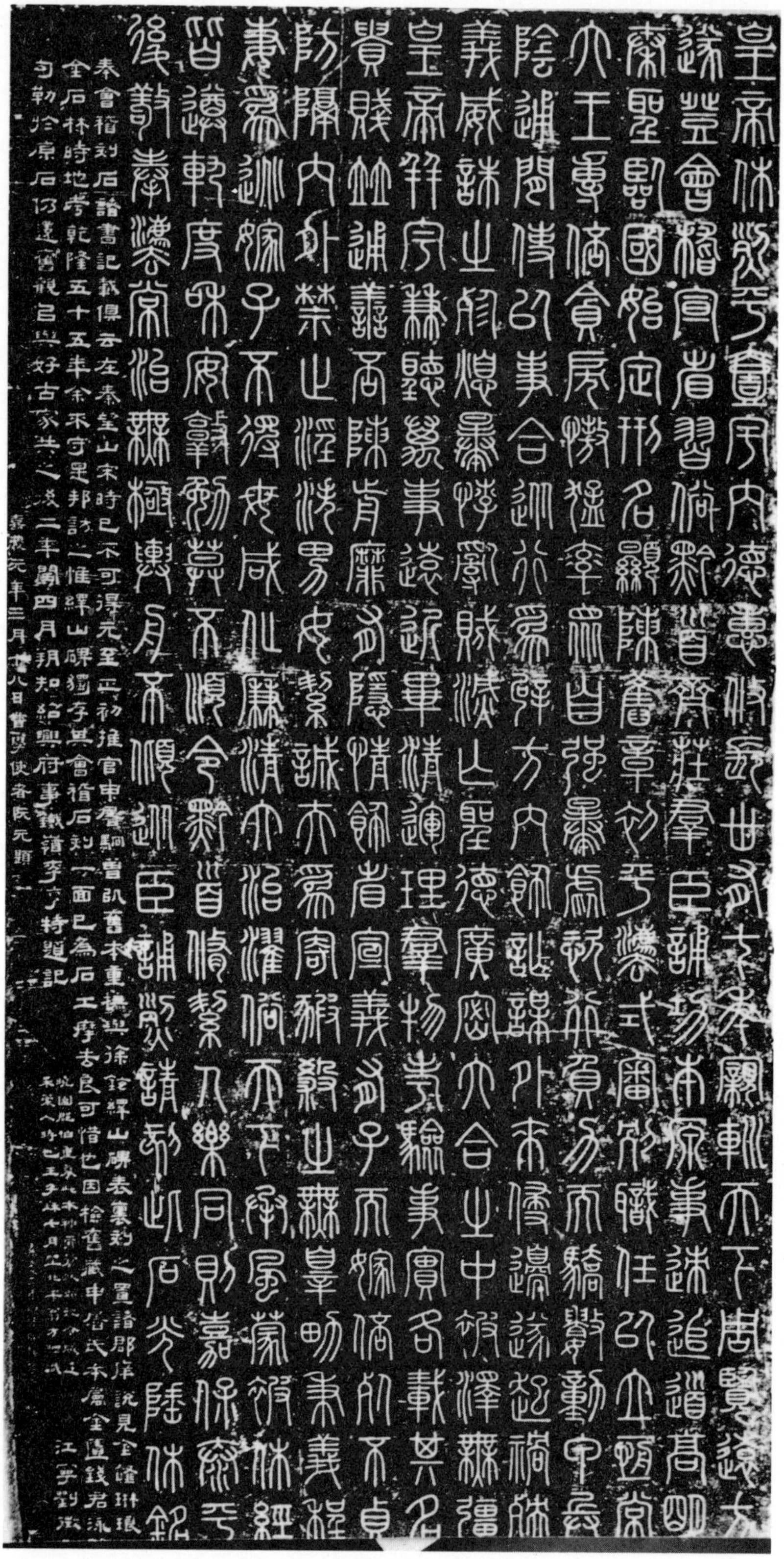

Huiji stone inscription, Qin Dynasty, (seal script).

Lishu

This form of Chinese script germinated in pre-Qin times. By the Qin Dynasty it came to be used by low-ranking officials in the Chinese government. It simplified the more complicated strokes of seal character script and used a bend instead of making a roundabout turn. *Lishu* is attributed to Cheng Miao, who lived in the state of Qin. The script was used by clerks working in prisons, hence the Chinese term *lishu* (servitude script). By the Han Dynasty it was promoted as a writing style. In over four hundred years of propagation *lishu* created many schools of writing. To facilitate writ-

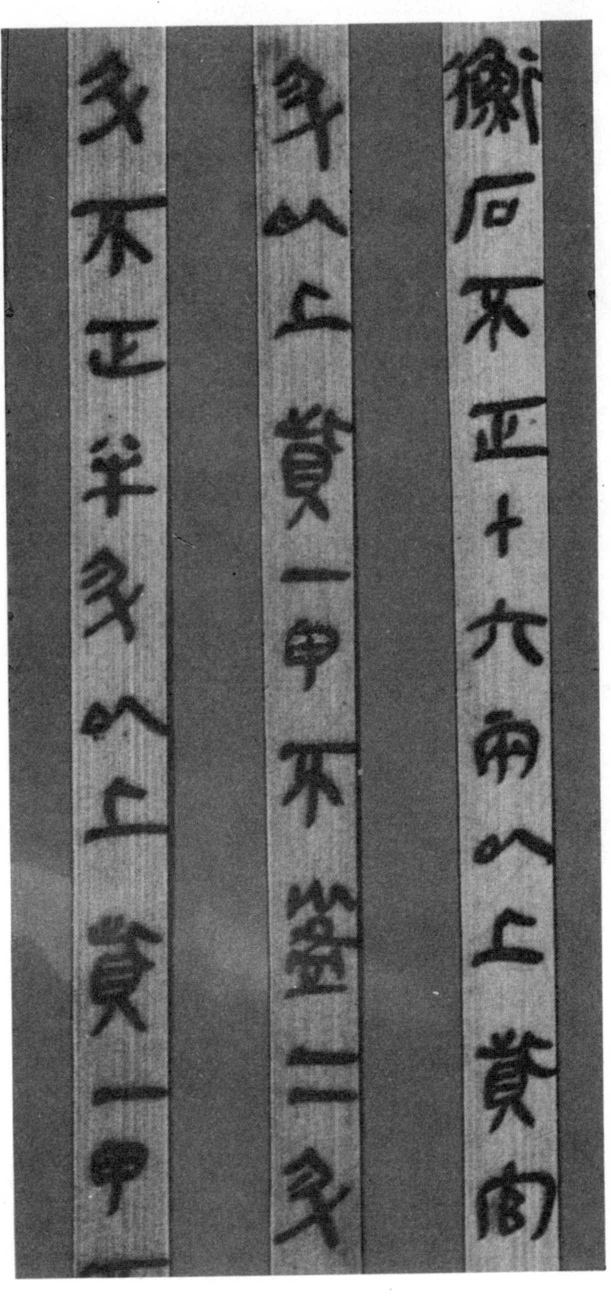

Statute's written on bamboo slips, Qin Dynasty, (classical script).

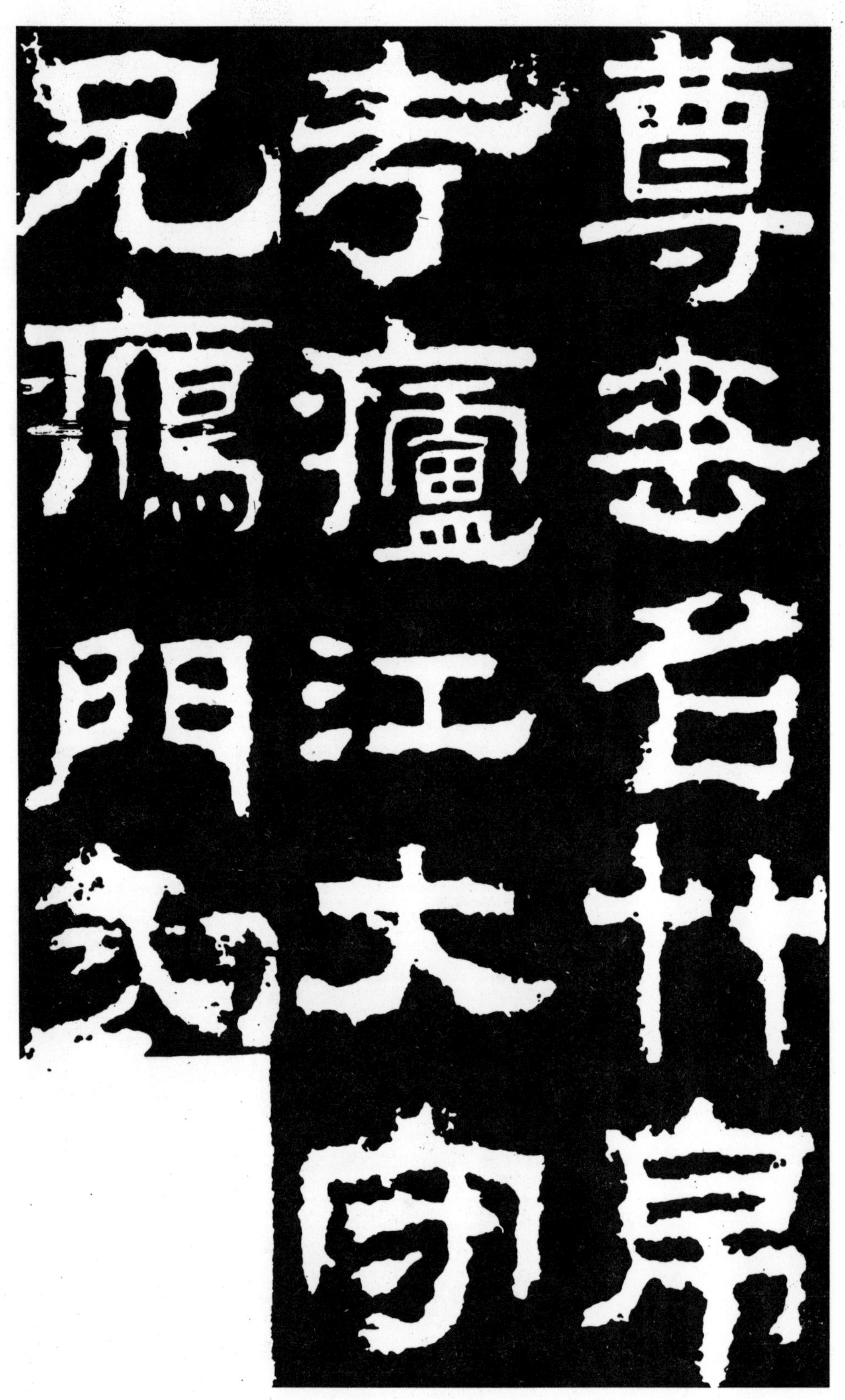

Heng Fang Stele, Han Dynasty, (classical script).

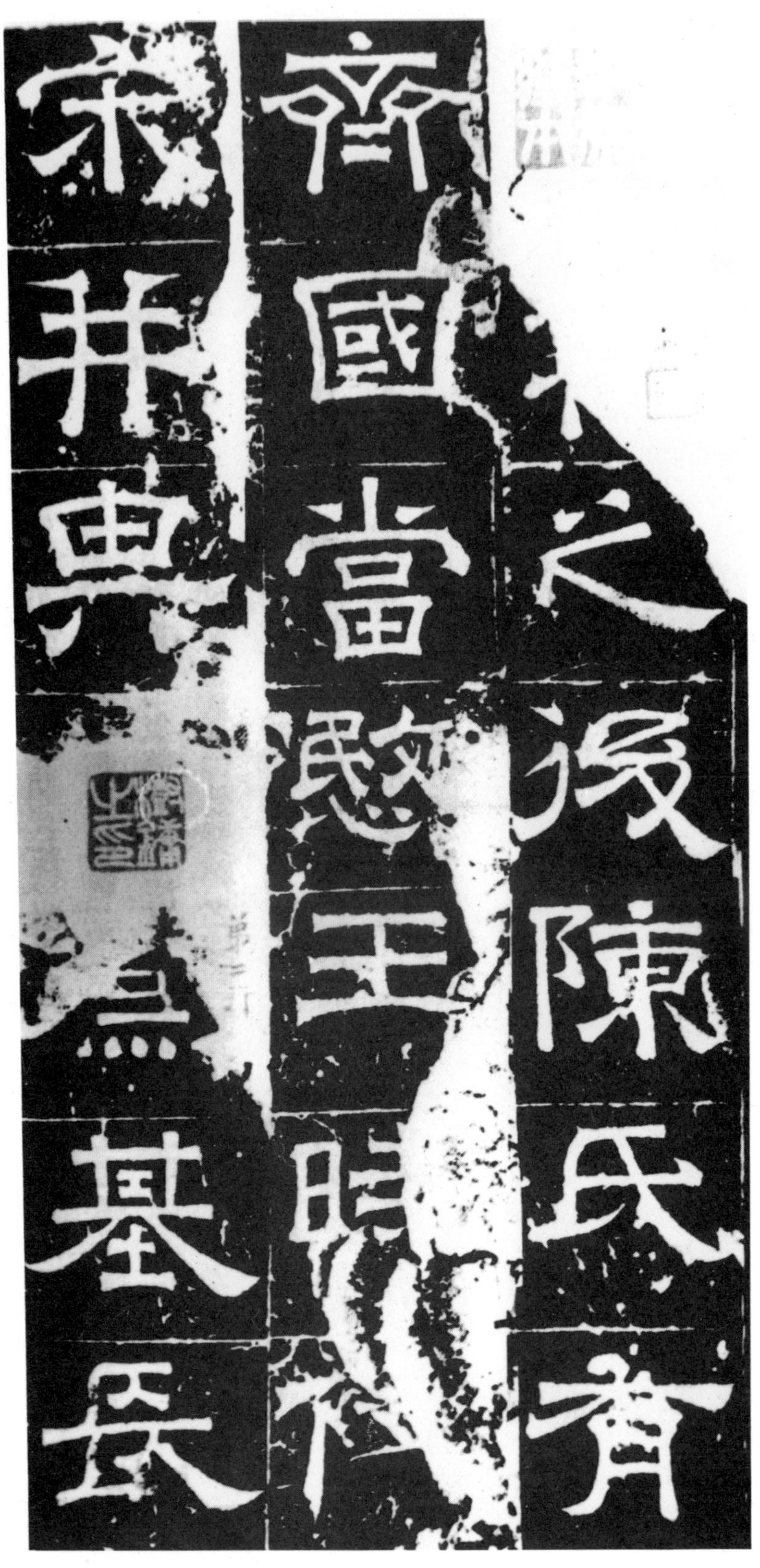

Cao Zhen Stele, Three Kingdoms Period, (classical script).

derwent a development of over four hundred years through the Wei, Jin, Southern and Northern dynasties. By the latter part of the Southern and Northern Dynasties the script rid itself of any remaining influence of *lishu*, attaining complete maturity.

Chinese calligraphy entered its golden age during the Sui and Tang dynasties, when China produced the largest number of calligraphers and made the greatest achievements in calligraphic art, unmatched by other historic periods or dynasties. I mentioned four schools of calligraphy before: Yan, Liu, Ou and Zhao. Of the four the first three thrived in the Tang Dynasty.

The above is a rough account of the history of Chinese calligraphy. The scripts ing, *lishu* branched out into *xingshu* (running script) and *caoshu* (cursive script), written in a flowing style with the strokes joined together. *Lishu* may be said to be the harbinger of running and cursive scripts.

Kaishu

Kaishu came into use in China at the end of the Han Dynasty. It is still used in China today after more than 1,700 years. It is the main Chinese writing style, called *kaishu*, or regular script. It is also called *zhengshu* or *zhenshu*.

Kaishu was initiated by Wang Cizhong toward the end of the Han Dynasty, according to legend. In the Wei-Jin period Zhong You (151-230) and Wang Xizhi (303-361) initiated a new way of writing that allowed *kaishu* and *lishu* to separate and form two systems. Chinese script un-

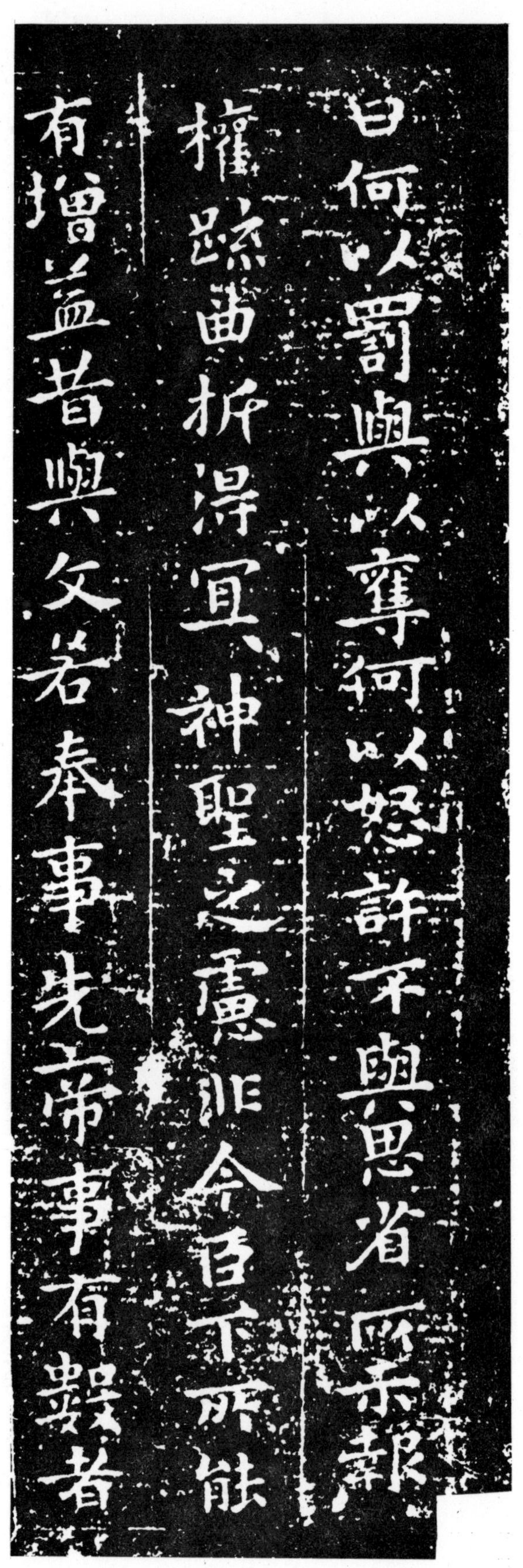

Zhong You, "Xuanshi Memorial to the Emperor" Three Kingdoms Period, (regular script).

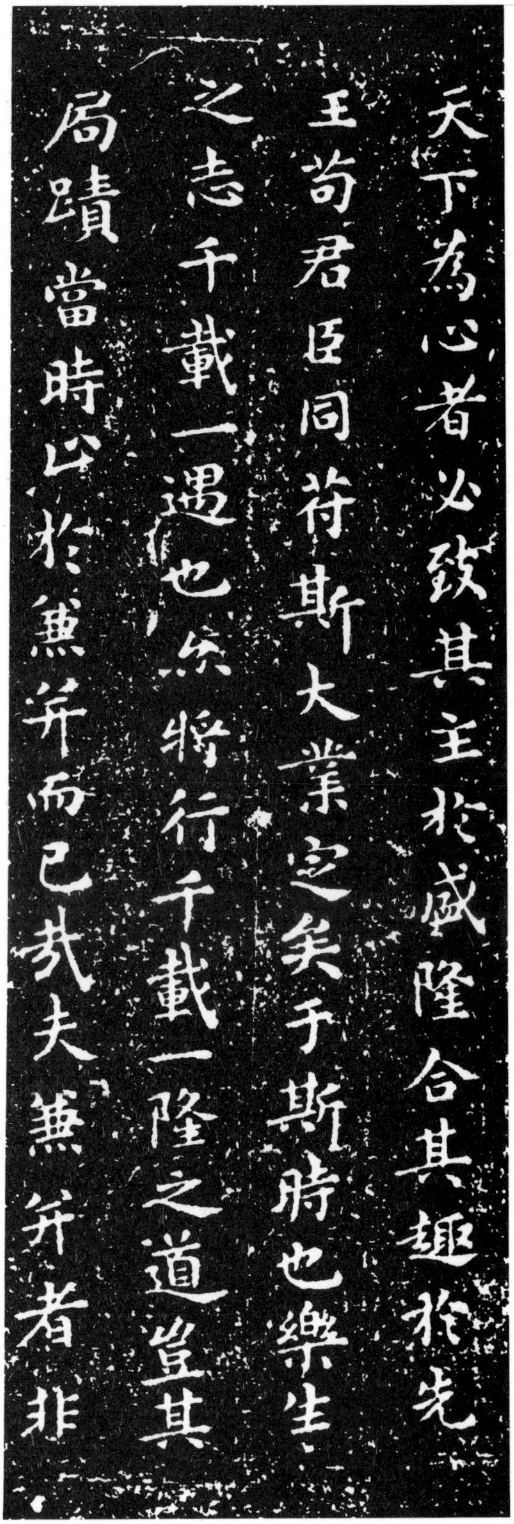

天下為心者必致其主於盛隆合其趣於先
王苟君臣同符斯大業定矣于斯時也樂生
之志千載一遇也亦將行千載一隆之道豈其
局蹟當時止於兼并而已哉夫兼并者非

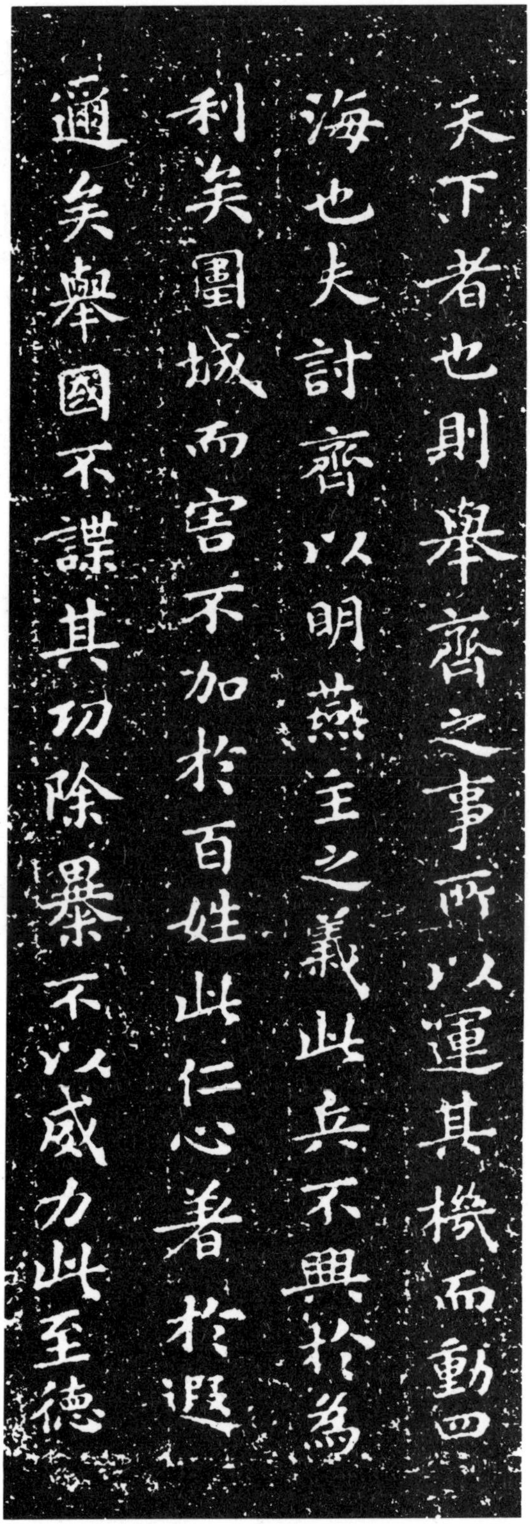

天下者也則舉齊之事所以運其機而動四
海也夫討齊以明燕主之義此兵不興於為
利矣圍城而害不加於百姓此仁心著於遐
邇矣舉國不謀其功除暴不以威力此至德

Wang Xizhi, "Yue Yi Lun," Jin Dynasty, (regular script).

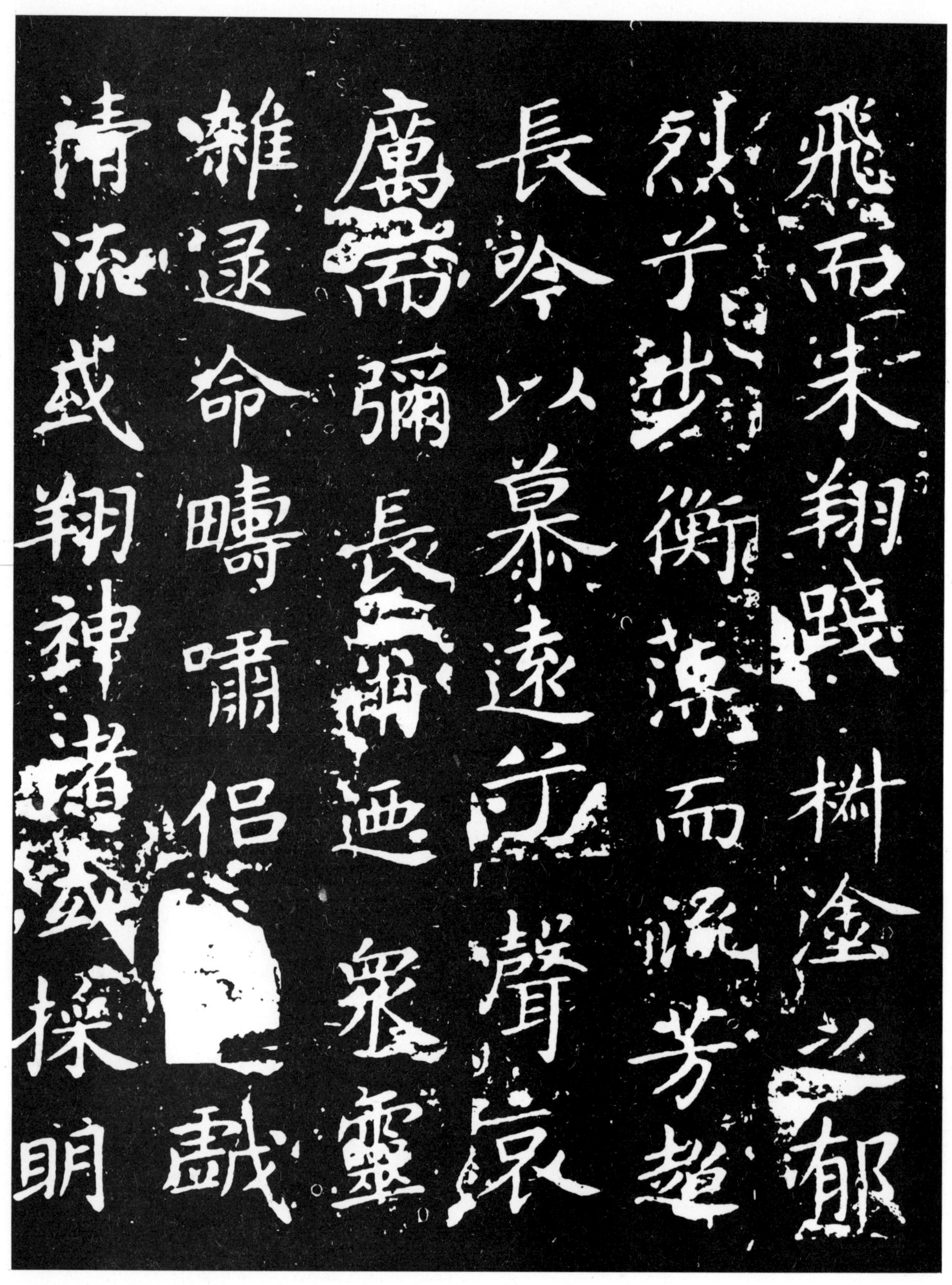

Wang Xianzhi, "*Fu* on the Goddess of the Luo River," Jin Dynasty, (regular script).

Cuan Longyan Stele, Liu Song Dynasty, (regular script).

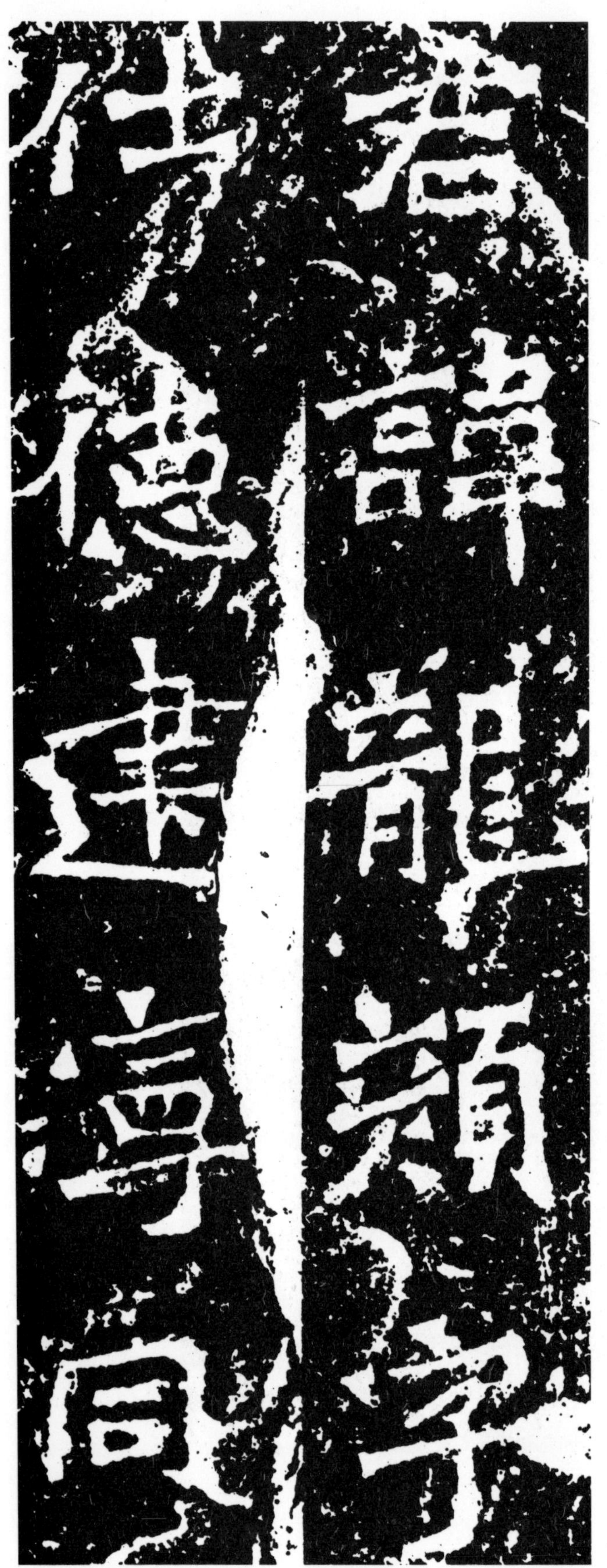

"On the Buddhist Images in the Lingzang Grotto of Longmen Grottos", Northern Wei Dynasty, (regular script).

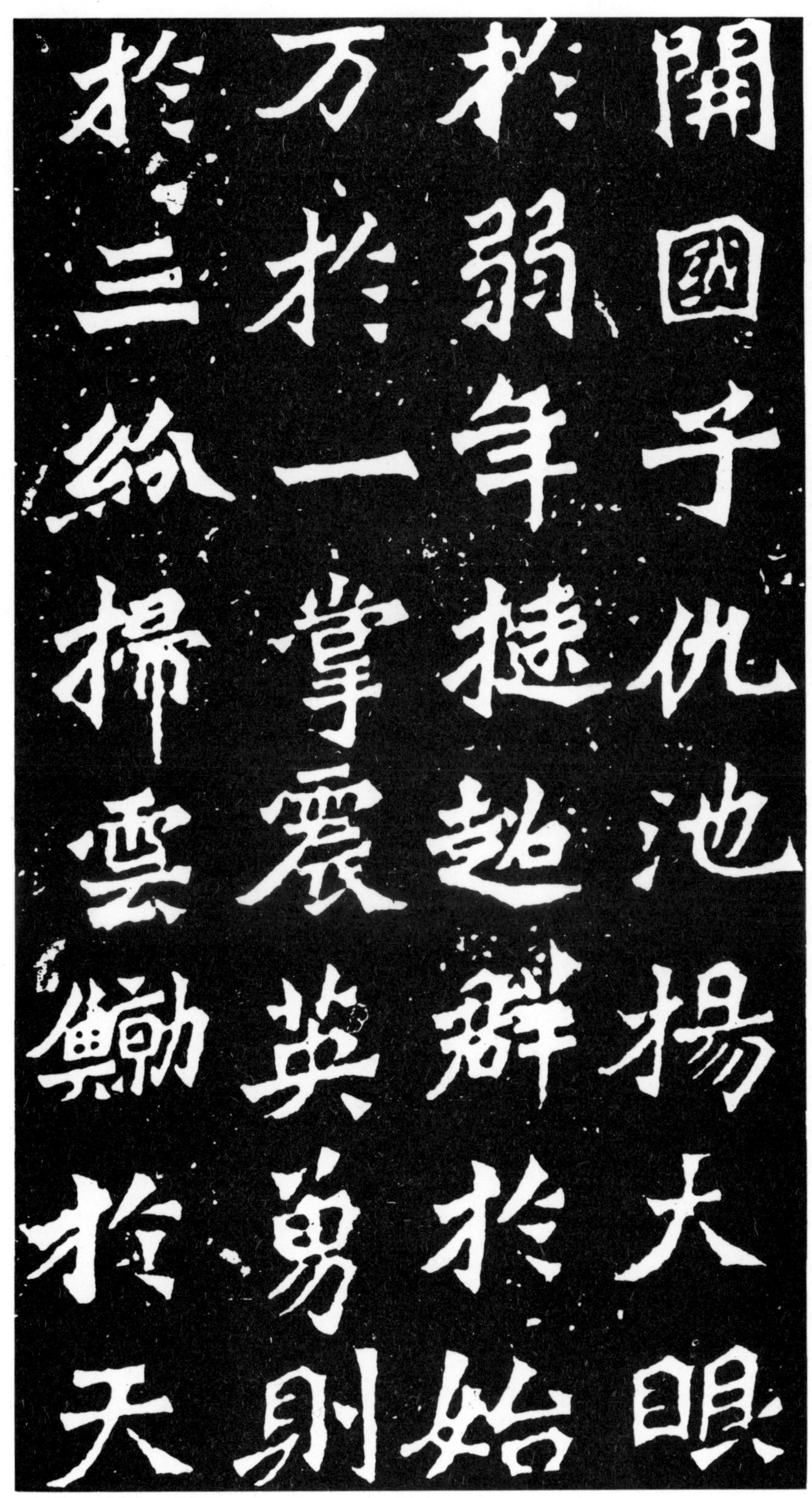

"On the Buddhist Images Erected by Yang Dayan", Northern Wei Dynasty, (regular script).

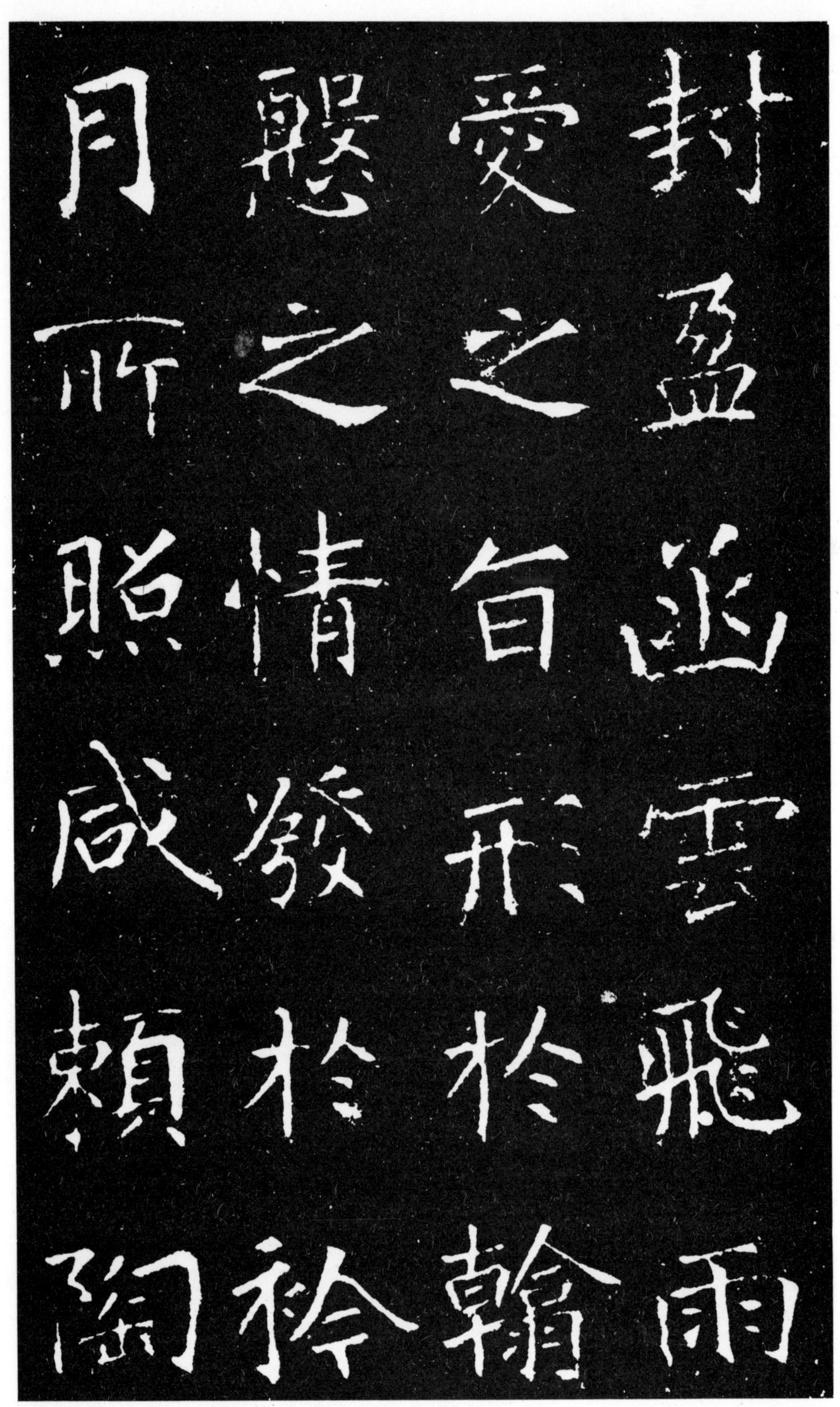

Long Zang Si Bei, (Commemorative Stone Tablet for the Long Zang Monastery), Sui Dynasty, (regular script).

龍文鼎輕天垂伏鼈海躍
長鯨解獻去佩書燼儒坑
纂堯中葉追尊大聖乃建

Yu Shinan, Stele in the Confucian Temple, Tang Dynasty (regular script).

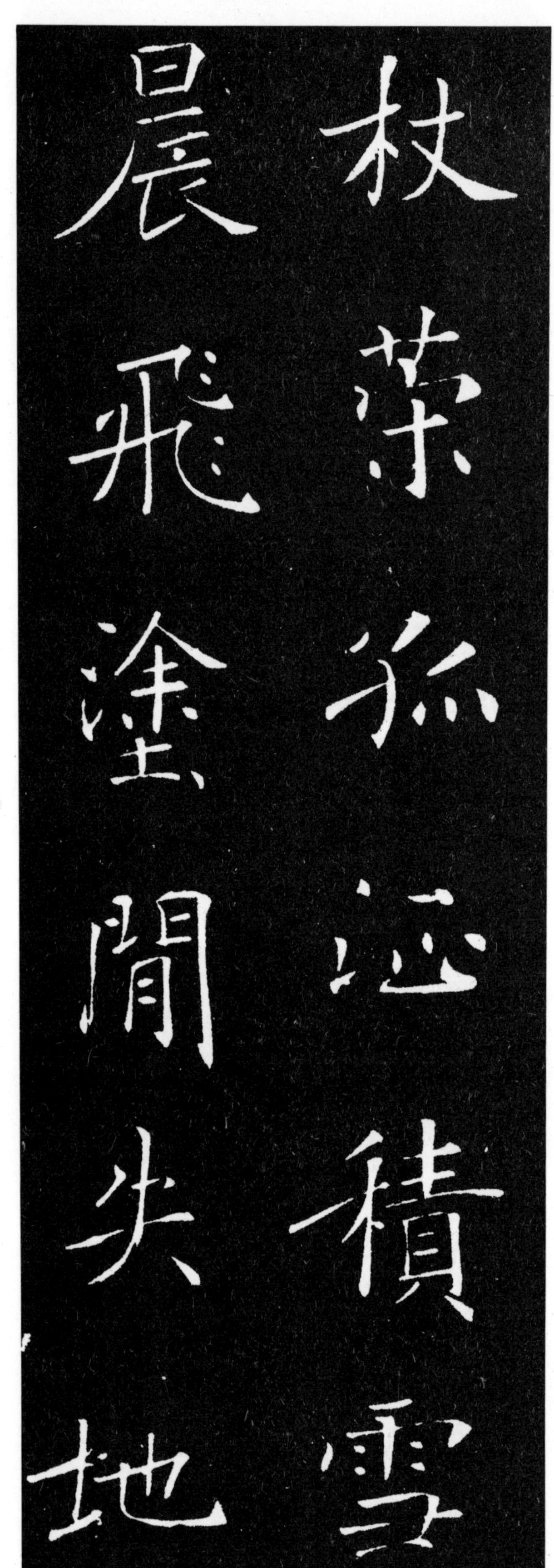

Chu Suiliang, *Yanta Shengjiao Xu* (Preface to the Holy Teaching of the Wild Goose Pagoda), Tang Dynasty (regular script).

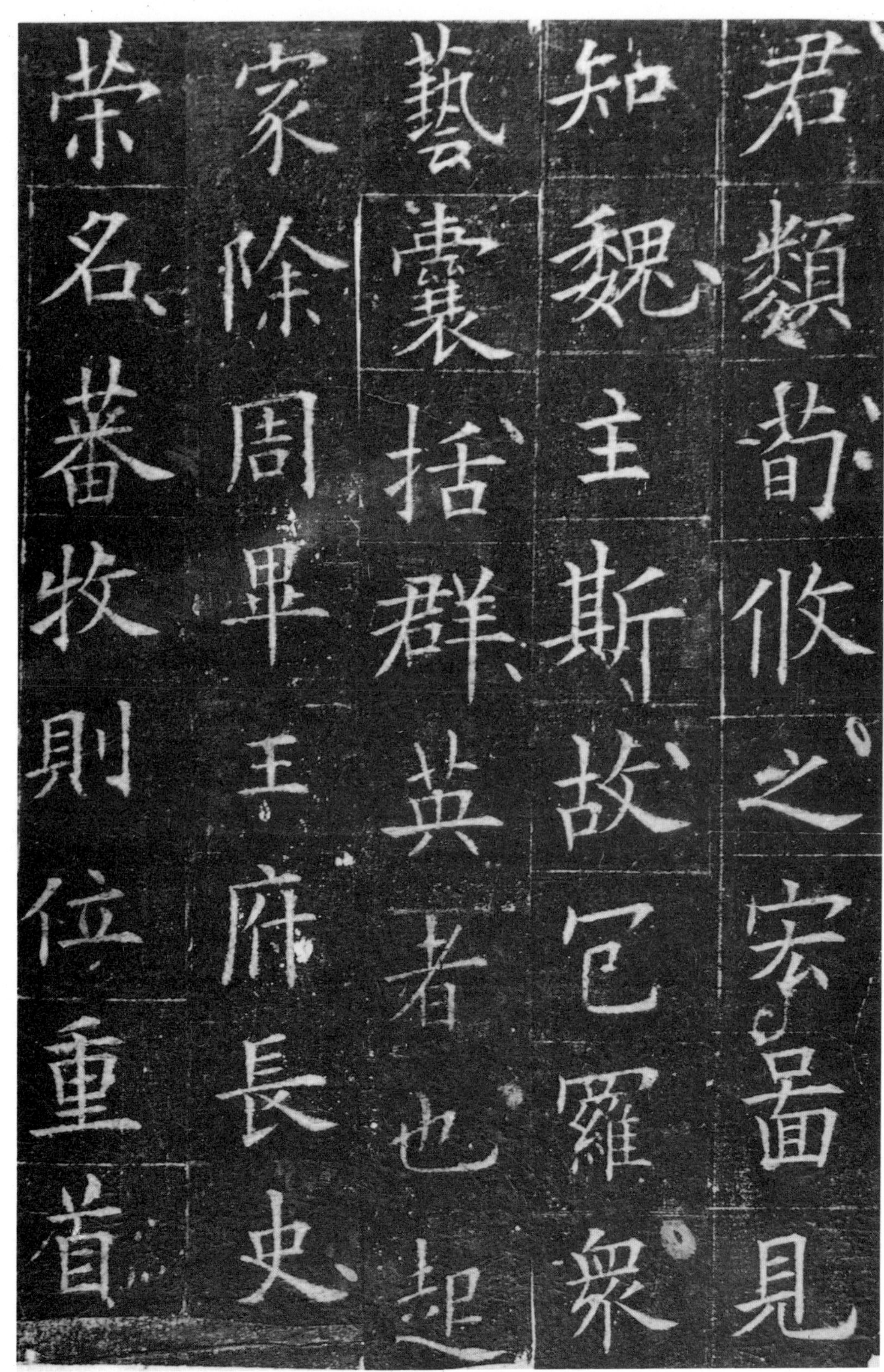

Ouyang Xun, Huangfu Dan Stele, Tang Dynasty (regular script).

刺史長樂恭侯橫劔
桂柯威重冠軍折瑞
蕃條聲高勃海公璋
邑中伯稟嵩山之秀
氣杼無蕭相降昴緯

趙思偘求諸寶坊驗以
所夢入寺見塔禮問禪
師聖夢有孚法名惟
肖其日賜錢五十萬絹
千匹助建修也則知精
一之行雖先天而不違

Yan Zhenqing, Duo Bao Pagoda Stele, Tang Dynasty (regular script).

宿山王映海蟻垤羣峯
嗟乎三界之沉寐久矣
佛以法華爲木鐸惟我
禪師超然深悟其皃也
岳瀆之秀冰雪之姿果
脣貝齒蓮目月面望之

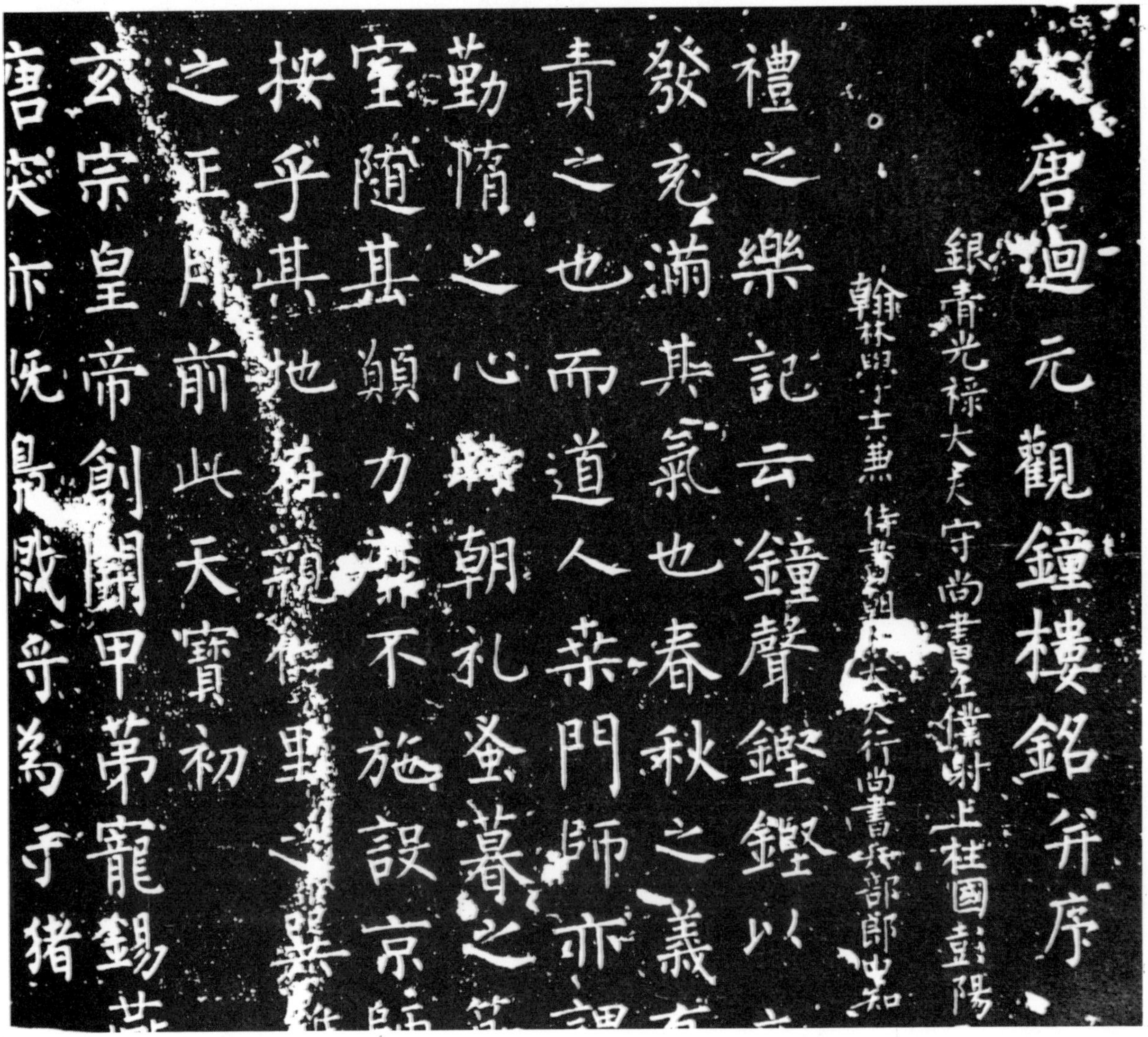

Liu Gongquan, Drum Tower, Inscription at the Huiyuan Taoist Temple, Tang Dynasty (regular script).

used today in China to serve the needs of society are *kaishu* (regular script) and *xingshu* (running script), but in the art arena *zhen*, *cao*, official script and seal character script compete with each other. They give a resplendent view of the beauty of calligraphy and the depth and breadth of this Oriental art, formed through several thousand years of ancient culture.

To study Chinese calligraphy, one should begin with *kaishu*. The next step is to study carefully various other scripts and absorb their good points. In this way one will create a unique style of one's own.

天地闔闢運乎鴻樞而乾坤爲之戶日月出入經乎黃道而卯酉爲之門是故建設琳宮摹寫玄象外則周垣之聯屬靈星之

Zhao Mengfu, *San Men di*, Yuan Dynasty (regular script).

Examples of regular script.
(at end of book)

美国
纽约
华盛顿
芝加哥
洛杉矶
旧金山
英格兰
澳大利亚
加拿大
开罗
火奴鲁鲁
中国

日本
法国
巴黎
瑞典
意大利
芬兰
西班牙
希腊
埃及
古巴
伊朗
波兰

亚当
艾米
安娜
本
卡尔
爱德华
大卫
埃伦
福克斯
艾德
艾琳
安德森
安德鲁
安吉尔
巴巴拉
本森
伯恩斯坦
贝蒂

吉姆
露西
保罗
迈克
乔治
汉斯
海伦
杰克
卡罗琳
卡特
卡瑟
克林顿
埃德加
爱迪生
爱因斯坦
伊丽莎白
简
简（珍妮）

布莱克
布什
卡贝尔
肯特
吉姆

约翰
乔伊
朱丽叶
琼
莱尔

图书在版编目(CIP)数据

中国书法入门:英文/郭伯南著.－北京:外文出版社,1995
ISBN 7－119－01435－8
Ⅰ.中… Ⅱ.郭… Ⅲ.汉字－书法－基本知识－英文 Ⅳ.J292.1

中国版本图书馆 CIP 数据核字(94)第 12771 号

中国书法入门
郭伯南　著
责任编辑　贾先锋
装帧设计　李士伋
*

外文出版社出版
(中国北京百万庄路 24 号)
邮政编码 100037
中国科学院印刷厂印刷
中国国际图书贸易总公司发行
(中国北京车公庄西路 35 号)
北京邮政信箱第 399 号　邮政编码 100044
1995 年(16 开)第一版
(英)
ISBN 7－119－01435－8/J.1263(外)
04000
84－E－754P